D1532729

chef's table

mountain flavors from asheville's most celebrated chefs

chef's table
mountain flavors from asheville's most celebrated chefs

Published by *Asheville Citizen-Times*

Copyright © 2008 by *Asheville Citizen-Times*
14 O. Henry Avenue
Asheville, North Carolina 28801
828-232-5934

Cover, Chef, and Food Photography © by
Asheville Citizen-Times.

Copyright permission granted for reprint of
chef and food photography by Southward Nowak of
Biltmore Estate and by Eric Scheffer of Savoy.

This cookbook is a collection of favorite recipes,
which are not necessarily original recipes.

All rights reserved. No part of this publication
may be reproduced in any form or by any means,
electronic or mechanical, including photocopying
and recording, or by any information storage or
retrieval system, without prior written permission
from *Asheville Citizen-Times.*

Library of Congress Control Number: 2007933995
ISBN: 978-0-9795052-0-1

Edited, Designed, and Manufactured by
Favorite Recipes® Press
An imprint of

FRP.

P. O. Box 305142
Nashville, Tennessee 37230
800-358-0560

Art Director: Steve Newman
Book Design: Dave Malone
Project Editor: Linda A. Jones

Manufactured in the United States of America
First Printing: 2008
7,000 copies

acknowledgments

Publisher: Jeffrey Green
Project Manager: Pam Weaver
Senior Photographer: Steve Dixon
Photographer: John Fletcher
Cover Design: Lena Richards
On-line: John Yenne, Michael Myers, Nate Ernst
Marketing: Luann Labedz, Tricia Speziale
Accounting: Andrea Morgan, Katrina Petrey,
    Elyse Giannetti, Joseph Nerney
Administration: Diane Robinson, Emily Thomas,
    Wayne Brigman
Proofing: Lisa Green, Susan Ihne, Sandie Rhodes,
    Katie McIntosh
IT: Josh Dillingham

Photographs printed with permission: Savoy and
Biltmore Estate.

Cover photograph by Steve Dixon. Cover
photography shot from Deltec Model Homes
now located at Mars Hill, North Carolina.
(www.deltechomes.com)

Recipes were written by chefs for restaurant use.
Recipes were tested on a sporadic basis; however,
the chef-written recipes may bear some
inconsistencies. The *Asheville Citizen-Times* and
the Asheville Independent Restaurant Association
are not responsible for errors in the recipes.

table of contents

introduction

I came to Asheville by way of Cape Town, East Lansing, Milwaukee, Madison, Winston-Salem, Tampa, and Honolulu—so I've been in some great food towns. But none of those places has presented such a variety of restaurants close at hand as Asheville. For lunch or dinner, I can walk outside of my office and reach ten or more restaurants of many styles, menus, and history.

I have a personal quest for good food and drink, so I want to share fifty of our local dining venues with you. Use this cookbook as a travel guide, a dining guide, a cooking experience, or as a memento of a visit to our lovely part of the mountains.

Asheville is a unique city nestled within the Blue Ridge Mountains of Western North Carolina. The *Asheville Citizen-Times* has been a part of this community and region since 1870. During our 137 years, we have been witness to Asheville's conception, renovation, and rise to be one of the nation's best in many ways: retirement, vacation destination, family life, and, we think, dining.

One of Asheville's many charms is the dining throughout our region. We boast that the independent businessperson can thrive in our region. The fifty restaurants featured in our cookbook are vastly different—barbecue, fine dining, local ingredients, custard, historical destinations, and a few local bars—but they all have one thing in common: independent ownership.

Most of our participating restaurants belong to Asheville Independent Restaurant Association (AIR); they are designated within their chapter. A portion of our sales will go toward their scholastic fund with the culinary program at Asheville-Buncombe Technical Community College. Please use AIR's Web site at www.airasheville.org and visit each restaurant. You will not be disappointed and likely will want to visit more than once!

I hope to see you at dinner tonight.

Jeffrey P. Green

President and Publisher

Asheville Citizen-Times

chef's table

12 Bones

Owners

Tom Montgomery and Sabra Kelley

5 Riverside Drive
Asheville, North Carolina 28801
828-253-4499
www.12bones.com
Hours: Lunch only (call for hours)

12 Bones graces the River Arts District of Asheville with a casual, laid-back style of dining for lunch and early dinner. Take-out service is available.

Many of the side items might seem a little unconventional at first. But when they come together, their flavors are complementary and harmonious. This is achieved by using simple ingredients and preparations.

Remember: Fat is flavor. Not sure who said that first, but 12 Bones gladly honors its sentiment. Butter is good, bacon is good...the list goes on and on. Don't be afraid of sugar or salt either; life is too short. On that note, try the Booty Bars recipe first.

booty bars

Preheat the oven to 350 degrees. Cream the butter, brown sugar, eggs and bananas in a mixing bowl. Add the flour, baking powder, baking soda and salt and mix just until the dough comes together. Stir in the chocolate chips. Spread in two 9×13-inch baking pans sprayed with nonstick cooking spray. Bake for 15 minutes or until light brown and the top springs back to the touch. Decorate with chocolate glaze, if desired.

2 cups (4 sticks) butter, softened
4 cups packed light brown sugar
8 eggs
6 bananas, mashed
6 cups all-purpose flour
2 teaspoons baking powder
2 teaspoons baking soda
1 teaspoon salt
3 cups miniature semisweet
    chocolate chips

Makes 40 bars

mashed sweet potatoes

Peel the sweet potatoes and cut into chunks. Place in a large saucepan and cover with water. Cook until the sweet potatoes are soft; drain. Combine the sweet potatoes, butter, cheese, cream, brown sugar, chili powder and salt in a mixing bowl and beat with the paddle attachment of an electric mixer until smooth.

5 pounds sweet potatoes
1/2 cup plus 2 tablespoons butter
1/2 cup plus 2 tablespoons grated
    Parmesan cheese
1/4 cup cream
1/4 cup packed brown sugar
1 1/2 teaspoons chili powder
1 1/2 teaspoons salt

Serves 10

12 Bones

chef's table
mountain flavors

chef's table

12 Bones

14

mushroom salad

To prepare the mushrooms, combine the vinegar, olive oil, mustard, onion, garlic, brown sugar, pepper and salt in a 6-quart container and blend with a hand blender until emulsified. Stir in the mushrooms. Marinate at room temperature for up to 1 hour; drain. Preheat the smoker to 200 degrees. Smoke the mushrooms using the manufacturer's directions for smoking vegetables.

To prepare the pesto, process the basil, garlic, sun-dried tomatoes, sunflower seeds, cheese and salt in a blender until coarsely chopped. Add the olive oil in a fine stream, processing constantly until blended. Do not over-blend. (This will make 1 cup.)

To prepare the salad, combine the smoked marinated mushrooms, the onion, bell pepper, 1/4 cup of the pesto, the Parmesan cheese, Worcestershire sauce, lemon juice and salt in a bowl and stir to mix. Serve at room temperature or chilled.

Note: Store the remaining Sun-Dried Tomato Pesto in the refrigerator to use for another purpose.

Smoked Marinated Mushrooms

1 cup balsamic vinegar

3/4 cup blended olive oil

1 tablespoon prepared mustard

1 tablespoon each minced yellow onion and garlic

2 tablespoons brown sugar

1 teaspoon pepper

1 1/2 teaspoons salt

2 pounds button mushrooms

Sun-Dried Tomato Pesto

2 ounces fresh basil

1 1/2 garlic cloves, peeled

1/4 cup sun-dried tomato halves

1 tablespoon sunflower seeds

1/3 cup grated Parmesan cheese

1 teaspoon salt

1/2 cup olive oil

Salad

1/4 white onion, julienned

1/2 red bell pepper, julienned

2 tablespoons shredded Parmesan cheese

1 teaspoon Worcestershire sauce

Juice of 1/2 lemon

1 teaspoon salt

Serves 10

chef's table

Amici Trattoria

Owner/Chef

Heath Miles

900 Hendersonville Road
Suite 201
Asheville, North Carolina 28803
828-277-1010
www.amiciasheville.com
Hours: Lunch: Monday – Friday
11:00 a.m. – 2:00 p.m.;
Dinner: Monday – Saturday 5:00 p.m.
Please call for reservations.
AIR member

Heath Miles began his professional culinary career in Atlanta at the five-star, five-diamond Ritz Carlton. He then joined Atlanta's The Fifth Group as sous chef for the opening of an innovative restaurant, The Food Studio.

Shortly thereafter, he helped create and build the concept and menu for the company's newest endeavor, La Tavola Trattoria, where he was named executive chef.

Miles left Atlanta to return home to Pittsburgh, Pennsylvania, as executive chef of Casbah, a Mediterranean, fine dining restaurant. While there, *Pittsburgh Magazine* recognized him as a Rising Star Chef.

A 1993 graduate of the Culinary Institute of America, Miles served an internship at the Grand Wailea Resort on Maui, where he trained under Chef Kathleen Daelemans, Food TV host and best-selling cookbook author. Upon graduation, Miles was accepted into the prestigious culinary apprentice program at the legendary Greenbrier Resort in West Virginia.

caesar dressing

Process the anchovies, Dijon mustard, garlic, vinegar, lemon juice, egg yolks and cheese in a food processor until puréed. Add the olive oil in a steady stream, processing constantly. Season with salt and pepper.

5 anchovies
1 teaspoon Dijon mustard
4 garlic cloves
3/4 cup white vinegar
1/4 cup lemon juice
3 pasteurized egg yolks
1/2 cup (2 ounces) grated
   Parmesan cheese
2 1/4 cups extra-virgin olive oil
Salt and pepper to taste

Makes about 4 cups

roasted butternut squash ravioli

Preheat the oven to 350 degrees. Spread the butter over the squash halves and sprinkle with salt and pepper. Place on a baking sheet and bake for 1 hour or until tender. Scrape the squash out of the shells and chop. Mix the ricotta cheese, sage, egg and Parmesan cheese in a mixing bowl. Stir in the squash, salt and pepper.

Place a dollop of the squash mixture in the center of each pasta square. Brush the edges with water and fold over, pressing to seal. Cook in boiling water in a large saucepan until the ravioli rises to the top. Drain and serve.

1 tablespoon butter
1 butternut squash, cut into
   halves lengthwise and deseeded
Salt and pepper to taste
1/2 cup ricotta cheese
1 tablespoon sage
1 egg
1/2 cup (2 ounces) grated
   Parmesan cheese
Fresh pasta sheets, cut into
   squares (available at specialty
   food stores)

Makes a variable amount

chef's table

Amici Trattoria

18

bolognese

Brown the ground beef and ground veal in a stockpot, stirring until crumbly; drain. Remove the beef mixture from the stockpot and set aside. Sauté the puréed pancetta in the stockpot. Add the onion and sweat. Add the beef mixture and the wine and cook until the wine evaporates. Crush the tomatoes and add to the mixture. Add the celery and carrot. Bring to a simmer. Cook until the mixture is reduced and thick. Add the cream and seasonings. Cook until reduced and thick. Add the lemon zest and spoon over hot cooked pasta.

Photograph at left.

1 pound ground beef
1 pound ground veal
8 ounces pancetta, puréed
1 onion, chopped
1/2 cup red wine
1 (15-ounce) can tomatoes
1 rib celery, finely chopped
1 carrot, finely chopped
1 cup cream
1 tablespoon oregano
1 tablespoon thyme
1 teaspoon red pepper flakes
Salt and black pepper to taste
Zest of 1 lemon
Hot cooked pasta

Serves 8 to 10

panna cotta

Soften the gelatin in the water in a small bowl. Split the vanilla bean and scrape the inside into the cream in a saucepan, discarding the skin. Add the sugar and bring to a simmer. Cook until the sugar is dissolved, stirring constantly. Turn off the heat. Stir in the gelatin mixture until dissolved. Pour into eight disposable individual serving containers and chill for about 4 hours. Carefully remove from the containers and serve with fresh berries.

1 tablespoon unflavored gelatin
3 tablespoons water
1 vanilla bean
4 cups heavy cream
1/2 cup sugar
Fresh berries

Serves 8

chef's table
mountain flavors

Battery Park Bistro

Executive Chef

Nic Sanford

22 Battery Park Avenue
Asheville, North Carolina 28801
828-253-2158
Hours: Monday – Saturday
11:30 a.m. – 10:00 p.m.;
Sunday 9:30 a.m. – 3:00 p.m.
AIR member

When you're in the mood for good times and great cuisine, be sure to dine at Battery Park Bistro. It is in one of the area's most pleasant settings and is known for its delightful staff and superb cuisine.

The Battery Park Bistro is a place where people meet, relax, and have quality food. Open for lunch and dinner daily, the New York style restaurant showcases homemade soups, delicious appetizers, prime aged beef, fresh grilled tuna, wild salmon, and homemade desserts. The cellar maintains a variety of wines from California, France, Italy, South America, and Australia, many offered by the glass.

Battery Park Bistro has established itself as one of the area's favorite culinary destinations and is sure to offer you a pleasant and unique dining experience. Come to relax and enjoy Asheville.

french onion soup

Melt the butter in a large Dutch oven. Add the onions and cook over medium heat until translucent. Add the wine and flour and stir until the liquid is smooth. Increase the heat and gradually add the stock. Bring to a boil and reduce the heat. Season with salt and pepper.

2 cups (4 sticks) butter
6 to 8 yellow onions, sliced (depending on size)
1 cup red wine
1 cup all-purpose flour
1 3/4 gallons chicken stock
Salt and pepper to taste

Serves 16 to 20

chicken piccata

Pound the chicken with a meat mallet until thin. Dredge in flour to coat. Heat olive oil in a sauté pan over medium-high heat. Add the chicken and cook until light brown on both sides. Add the wine, stirring to deglaze the skillet. Add the garlic, capers, artichoke hearts, butter, lemon and salt. Reduce the heat to medium and add the basil. Discard the lemon slices. Serve over the linguini.

4 boneless skinless chicken breasts
All-purpose flour for dredging
Olive oil for sautéing
1/2 cup white wine
1/4 cup minced fresh garlic
1/4 cup small capers
6 artichoke hearts, sliced
1/4 cup (1/2 stick) butter, sliced
1 lemon, thinly sliced
Salt to taste
1/4 cup fresh basil, chiffonade
1 pound linguini, cooked

Serves 4

Battery Park Bistro

chef's table

Battery Park Bistro

22

maryland-style crab cakes with red pepper aïoli

To prepare the aïoli, process the mayonnaise, bell peppers, basil, lemon juice and garlic in a food processor. Season with salt and pepper.

To prepare the crab cakes, whip the eggs, Dijon mustard, onion, bell pepper, horseradish, lemon juice, tarragon, parsley and mayonnaise in a bowl. Fold in the crab meat gently, being careful not to shred the crab meat. Measure 1/2 cup of the crab meat mixture at a time and press the bread crumbs on the outside only. Shape into patties and place on a baking sheet. Chill for 2 hours or longer.

Preheat the oven to 400 degrees. Heat a small amount of butter in an ovenproof skillet over high heat. Add the crab cakes and cook only until brown on each side. Bake for 10 minutes or until cooked through. Serve with the aïoli.

red pepper aïoli

2 cups mayonnaise
3 red bell peppers, roasted and
    peeled
6 tablespoons fresh basil
1 tablespoon lemon juice
3/4 tablespoon minced fresh garlic
Salt and pepper to taste

crab cakes

5 eggs, beaten
1/2 cup Dijon mustard
1/2 cup finely chopped
    yellow onion
1/2 cup finely chopped red
    bell pepper
2 tablespoons prepared horseradish
1/4 cup lemon juice
2 tablespoons dried tarragon
2 tablespoons fresh parsley
1 cup (about) mayonnaise
5 pounds fresh lump crab meat,
    shells removed
3 cups (about) finely crushed
    bread crumbs
Butter

Makes 10 to 12 crab cakes

chef's table
mountain flavors

Bier Garden

Chef
Joel Meadows

46 Haywood Street
Asheville, North Carolina 28801
828-285-0002
www.ashevillebiergarden.com
Hours: Daily 11:00 a.m. – 2:00 a.m.
AIR member

The Bier Garden opened in 1994 and has become one of Asheville's favorite restaurants, with the best beer selection in Western North Carolina. It is conveniently located on historic Haywood Street in the heart of Asheville's downtown shopping district.

The Bier Garden takes pride in an extensive selection of beers from around the world. There's a beer for every beer lover with a selection of over two hundred beers, including some local microbrews.

Complementing the beers is an extensive food menu featuring American fusion cuisine created by award-winning chef Joel Meadows. Offerings include a large selection of appetizers, soups and salads, burgers and sandwiches, as well as a children's menu. For dinner, enjoy the fine dining menu with daily chef specials in addition to some favorite menu regulars.

sunflower pesto

Process the sunflower seeds, basil, garlic, olive oil and Parmesan cheese in a food processor until blended to the desired consistency.

6 pounds sunflower seeds, salted
  and shelled
4 ounces fresh basil,
  stems removed
1/4 cup fresh garlic
2 quarts extra-virgin olive oil
1/4 cup (1 ounce) grated
  Parmesan cheese or
  asiago cheese

Makes 3 quarts

The Blue Ridge Parkway stretches 469 miles, starting in Virginia's Shenandoah National Park, running right through the mountains of Asheville, and ending at Cherokee. With some twenty-one million visitors a year, it is the most visited National Park Service site in the country.

The parkway is a great place to take a scenic drive, go for a hike, watch for wildlife, or stop for a picnic. While any grassy place along the parkway will do, the following are some good choices for spreading out a picnic feast:

Waterrock Knob, Milepost 451; Devil's Courthouse Overlook, Milepost 422; Graveyard Fields, Milepost 418.8; Mount Pisgah picnic area, Milepost 407.8; Folk Art Center, Milepost 382; Craggy Gardens picnic area, Milepost 367.6; Mount Mitchell State Park, Milepost 355; Linn Cove Visitor Center, Milepost 304; Price Lake, Milepost 296; Moses H. Cone Memorial Park, Milepost 292.7.

For more information on the Blue Ridge Parkway, visit www.nps.gov/blri.
　　　　　　　　　　　　　　—Karen Chávez, Asheville Citizen-Times

chef's table

Bier Garden

26

guinness stew

Sear the beef in a stockpot with the bacon, garlic and brown sugar.
Add the stout and stir to deglaze the stockpot. Stir in the broth. Add
the onions, carrots, parsnips, kale and potatoes. Simmer for 3 hours.
Add the rosemary and thyme and simmer for 30 minutes. Season with
salt and white pepper. Add enough arrowroot to thicken to the
desired consistency, stirring constantly.

5 pounds cube sirloin steak
2 pounds apple smoked bacon
6 ounces garlic, minced
1 (1-pound) package
* brown sugar*
6 quarts Guinness stout
3 gallons beef broth
4 pounds yellow onions, chopped
4 pounds carrots, chopped
5 pounds parsnips, sliced
5 pounds kale, coarsely chopped
5 pounds red potatoes, cut into
* quarters*
1/2 cup fresh rosemary, chopped
5 ounces fresh thyme
Salt and white pepper to taste
Arrowroot or all-purpose flour
* for thickening*

Serves 8 to 10

Bier Garden

chef's table

Biltmore Estate

Chef

Rick Boyer

Biltmore Estate

1 Approach Road
Asheville, North Carolina 28803
800-624-1575 or 828-225-1333
www.biltmore.com
Hours: Hours vary by restaurant.
Please call to confirm operation hours.

Biltmore has five restaurants on the estate. The Dining Room at the Inn on Biltmore Estate, where Chef Rick Boyer is known for his Carolina Crab Cakes and other delectable dishes, opened March 16, 2001. The 150-seat restaurant specializes in regional cuisine with menus inspired by estate-raised beef, lamb, and produce complemented by estate wines. Gourmet dining is offered in an elegant atmosphere with white tablecloths, Vanderbilt china, crystal, and an attentive wait staff. The little luxuries and attention to detail that characterize Vanderbilt entertaining add up to make an evening to remember.

The fried calamari can be enjoyed at Bistro, adjacent to Biltmore Winery, the most visited in the United States. Although Executive Chef Edwin French ensures the dishes reflect the flavors of the Blue Ridge Mountains, guests at Bistro could think they have stepped into a café somewhere in Provence or Tuscany. Tables surround an open kitchen where each day's harvest is sautéed and stirred, grilled and flavored with the themes of the region.

fried calamari with olive salad and provençale sauce

To prepare the sauce, preheat the oven to 350 degrees. Core the tomatoes. Place on a baking sheet with sides and drizzle with 1/4 cup canola oil. Sprinkle with salt and pepper. Roast for 30 minutes. Add the whole garlic and shallots and toss to mix. Bake for 15 minutes. Remove from the oven to cool. Process the tomato mixture, anchovy and roasted bell pepper in a blender until puréed. Strain the mixture into a bowl, discarding the pulp. Add the lemon zest, lemon juice, cheese, basil and oregano and blend with an immersion blender. Add the oil in a fine stream, processing until emulsified. Season with salt and pepper. (This will make 2 cups.)

To prepare the calamari, preheat oil in a deep fryer to 350 degrees. Dredge the squid in seasoned flour to coat, shaking off the excess. Fry in the hot oil until crispy, being careful not to overcook. Place in a warm bowl and top with the Olive Salad and 1/4 cup of the Tomato Provençale Sauce.

Note: Store the remaining Tomato Provençale Sauce in the refrigerator to use for another purpose.

provençale sauce

8 ounces Roma tomatoes
1/4 cup canola oil
Salt and pepper to taste
2 tablespoons fresh garlic
1/4 cup sliced shallots
1 anchovy
1/4 cup chopped roasted red
    bell pepper
Zest and juice of 1 lemon
2 tablespoons grated
    Parmigiano-Reggiano cheese
1 tablespoon chopped fresh basil
1/2 tablespoon fresh oregano
3/4 cup canola oil

calamari

Vegetable oil for deep-frying
1 pound squid, tentacles and tails
Seasoned all-purpose flour
1 cup Olive Salad (page 31)
1/4 cup Tomato Provençale Sauce

Serves 4 to 6

Biltmore Estate

carolina crab cakes

Preheat the oven to 325 degrees. Mix all the ingredients except the olive oil in a medium bowl. Shape tightly into balls and flatten gently. Place on a baking sheet lined with baking parchment and sprinkled with additional bread crumbs. Heat a medium skillet over medium heat and add the olive oil. Add four or five crab cakes at a time and cook until golden brown on the bottom. Turn the cakes and cook for 1 minute longer. Remove to a baking sheet lined with baking parchment. Bake for 15 minutes or until cooked through. Serve immediately.

Photograph at left.

2 pounds pasteurized jumbo lump
    crab meat, shells removed
2 eggs
1/4 cup Japanese-style bread
    crumbs, or as needed to bind
    the crab cakes
2 tablespoons minced chives
Juice of 1/2 lemon
1/3 cup mayonnaise
1 1/2 tablespoons each Dijon mustard
    and whole grain mustard
1 tablespoon Old Bay seasoning
Salt and pepper to taste
2 tablespoons mild olive oil
    or butter

Makes 6 to 8 crab cakes

olive salad

Pulse the kalamata olives, Spanish olives, chiles, capers, garlic, oil, vinegar, oregano and red pepper in a food processor to mix. Spoon into a serving bowl. Store in the refrigerator.

1/2 cup kalamata olives
1/2 cup Spanish olives
1 cup pepperoncini
2 tablespoons capers
1 teaspoon fresh garlic
2 tablespoons canola oil
1 teaspoon red wine vinegar
1 teaspoon fresh oregano
1/2 teaspoon crushed red pepper

Makes 2 cups

chef's table

mountain flavors

Bistro 1896

Head Chef

Amanda Hilty

Bistro 1896

7 Pack Square
Asheville, North Carolina 28801
828-251-1300
www.bistro1896.com
Hours: Lunch: Monday – Saturday
11:15 a.m. – 4:00 p.m.;
Dinner: Monday – Thursday and
Sunday 5:00 p.m. – 10:00 p.m.;
Friday and Saturday
5:00 p.m. – 10:30 p.m.;
Sunday Brunch: 10:30 a.m. – 4:00 p.m.

Bistro 1896 has become an Asheville landmark known for its broadly appealing menu and attentive service. Mixing the familiar with the unexpected, Bistro 1896's menu reflects Asheville's diversity by offering everything from braised short ribs and grape-leaf-wrapped salmon to velvety chicken potpie. Now in its tenth year, this venerable restaurant continues to draw crowds. Enjoy a full bar, dining on historic Pack Square, and late afternoon patio seating perfect for that second bottle of wine.

Located at the top of Pack Square in historic downtown Asheville, Bistro 1896 is within walking distance of local art galleries, museums, theaters, musical venues, and local shops. Ample parking is available.

cornmeal-crusted mountain trout

Mix the cornmeal, 1/2 tablespoon salt, 1 tablespoon black pepper and the cayenne pepper together. Dredge the trout in the cornmeal mixture. Panfry in the olive oil in a skillet for 2 minutes on each side. Remove the trout from the skillet and keep warm.

Add the apple, pear, onion, currants and walnuts to the drippings in the skillet and sauté for 1 minute or until the fruit is soft. Add the cream and cook until the cream is reduced by one-half. Remove from the heat. Swirl in the butter a small amount at a time until combined. Season with salt and black pepper. Place the trout on a serving plate and finish with the sauce.

Bistro 1896

1 cup cornmeal
1/2 tablespoon salt
1 tablespoon black pepper
1 tablespoon cayenne pepper
2 to 4 trout fillets
Olive oil for pan frying
1 Granny Smith apple, peeled
    and thinly sliced
1 pear, peeled and thinly sliced
1/4 cup julienned red onion
2 tablespoons currants
2 tablespoons walnut
    pieces, toasted
2 tablespoons heavy cream
1 cup (2 sticks) butter, softened
Salt and black pepper to taste

Serves 2 to 4

The Blue Ridge is a long escarpment running through the region to the South Carolina and Virginia lines. The top of the Blue Ridge is the Eastern Continental Divide. Waters on the east side the Divide flow to the Atlantic; waters to the West flow to the Gulf of Mexico.

—Jim Buchanan, Asheville Citizen-Times

chef's table

mountain flavors

Bistro 1896

fried green tomato napoleon with blackened ham

Preheat oil in a deep fryer. Mix cornmeal with salt and pepper in a shallow dish. Coat the tomatoes in flour. Dip in the beaten eggs and coat with the cornmeal mixture. Deep-fry in the hot oil until golden.

Sweat the ham, bell peppers, scallions, onion and mushrooms in 1 1/2 tablespoons butter with 2 teaspoons blackening spice in a skillet for 2 minutes. Add the cream and wine and cook until reduced to the desired consistency.

Dust the shrimp with additional blackening spice. Sear in 1/2 tablespoon butter in a skillet for 2 minutes on each side. To serve, layer the tomatoes with the ham mixture. Add the shrimp and top with goat cheese.

Bistro 1896

Vegetable oil for deep-frying
Cornmeal for coating
Salt and pepper to taste
3 green tomatoes, cored and
    sliced 1/4 inch thick
All-purpose flour for dusting
3 eggs, beaten
4 ounces country ham, julienned
1/4 cup finely chopped green
    bell pepper
1/4 cup finely chopped red
    bell pepper
1/4 cup sliced scallions
1/4 cup finely chopped red onion
1/4 cup finely chopped
    portobello mushrooms
1 1/2 tablespoons butter
2 teaspoons blackening spice
1 1/2 cups heavy cream
1/4 cup white wine
3 shrimp, peeled and deveined
Blackening spice for dusting
1/2 tablespoon butter
Crumbled goat cheese for topping

Serves 2 as an appetizer

chef's table

mountain flavors

Black Forest Restaurant

Chef/Owner

George Ettwein

2155 Hendersonville Road
Asheville, North Carolina 28704
828-687-7980
www.blackforestasheville.com
Hours: Serving dinner daily 4:00 p.m.;
seasonal and weekend deck hours.

"Fine food, impeccable service at Black Forest Restaurant."

—*Asheville Citizen-Times* review

Award-winning Euro-American cuisine awaits you in South Asheville's premier restaurant, specializing in German, Italian, steaks, and seafood. Bring your friends and enjoy our warm chalet-style ambiance or visit the fireside lounge with adjoining deck area for that relaxing summer or winter dining experience you will be sure to talk about.

Celebrating its tenth year with seven dining rooms for parties from ten to two hundred, owners George, Greg, Bill, and Carol invite you to come and join the many others who have made the Black Forest their favorite place. Live music Friday and Saturday nights and seasonal weekend deck hours. Reservations recommended.

potato pancakes

Combine the potatoes, onion, eggs, flour, nutmeg, parsley and scallions in a bowl and mix well. Heat a well-oiled skillet over medium-high heat. Ladle a portion of the potato mixture at a time into the hot skillet and fry until brown on each side. To serve, top with sour cream and applesauce.

2 large potatoes, shredded
1/2 onion, finely chopped
2 eggs
3/4 cup all-purpose flour
1/2 teaspoon grated nutmeg
Chopped parsley
Chopped scallions
Sour cream
Applesauce

Makes 8

garlic-infused spinach

Remove the stems from the spinach and rinse the leaves thoroughly. Sauté the garlic in olive oil in a skillet until light brown. Add the spinach, wine, lemon juice, 1/2 cup cheese, salt and pepper and sauté until the spinach wilts. Garnish with lemon slices and additional cheese.

1 pound fresh spinach
  (4 ounces per person)
2 teaspoons finely chopped
  fresh garlic
Olive oil for sautéing
2 tablespoons white wine
1 teaspoon fresh lemon juice
1/2 cup (2 ounces) grated
  Parmesan cheese
Salt and pepper to taste
Lemon slices for garnish
Grated Parmesan cheese
  for garnish

Serves 4

chef's table
mountain flavors

chef's table

Black Forest Restaurant

38

ravioli aglio e olio

To prepare the aglio e olio, sauté the garlic and red pepper flakes in the olive oil in a skillet until the garlic is light brown. Remove from the heat. Stir in parsley to cool.

To prepare the pasta and assemble, cook the pasta using the package directions until al dente. Prepare the sauce using the package directions. Spoon the sauce onto each serving plate. Place the ravioli in the sauce. Top with the aglio e olio and sprinkle with the cheese.

Photograph at left.

aglio e olio

2 tablespoons chopped fresh garlic
2 teaspoons red pepper flakes
6 tablespoons extra-virgin olive oil
Chopped fresh parsley

ravioli and assembly

16 ravioli
Marinara or pomodoro sauce
Freshly grated pecorino
     Romano cheese

Serves 4

herb-seared mahi-mahi

Mix equal portions of tarragon, basil, oregano, dill, thyme and onion powder in a bowl. Brush fish with olive oil and sprinkle with the herb mixture. Heat olive oil in a skillet and add the fish. Cook for 3 minutes on each side or until brown. Add wine, stirring to deglaze the skillet. Finish the sauce with butter to thicken. Glaze the fish with the sauce.

Tarragon, basil, oregano, dill
     and thyme
Onion powder
Mahi-mahi fillets, skin removed
     (6 to 8 ounces per person)
Olive oil
White wine
Butter

Makes a variable amount

chef's table

mountain flavors

Blue Ridge Dining Room

Executive Chef

David Rowland

Grove Park Inn Resort and Spa

290 Macon Avenue
Asheville, North Carolina
828-252-2711
www.groveparkinn.com
Hours: Breakfast: 6:30 a.m. – 11:00 a.m.;
Sunday Brunch: 11:00 a.m. – 2:30 p.m.;
Dinner: 4:00 p.m. – 9:30 p.m.;
Lunch hours vary by season.
Resort Casual
AIR member

Savor selections from the menu or enjoy one of the bountiful weekend buffets while overlooking the Asheville skyline, the resort's gorgeous fairways, and, of course, the Dining Room's namesake, the Blue Ridge Mountains.

Experience the famous and award-winning Friday Night Seafood Buffet, Saturday Night Prime Rib Buffet, and Sunday Brunch.

The Blue Ridge Dining Room is inside The Grove Park Inn Resort and Spa.

duck breast with red-eye gravy

Season the duck with salt and pepper. Heat the oil in a skillet until hot. Add the duck skin side down and cook for 4 minutes on each side. Remove from the skillet and keep warm. Add the shallots and garlic to the pan drippings and sauté for 1 minute. Stir in the coffee, broth and thyme. Simmer for 15 minutes. Strain the mixture and return to the skillet. Cook until the liquid is reduced by one-half. Stir in the butter a small amount at a time to emulsify. Season with salt, pepper and brown sugar. Cut the duck into slices and serve with the gravy.

4 boneless duck breasts
Salt and pepper to taste
2 tablespoons vegetable oil
3 shallots, chopped
1 garlic clove, chopped
2 tablespoons coffee beans, ground
2 cups chicken broth
1/4 teaspoon dried thyme
2 tablespoons unsalted butter, cut into cubes
Pinch of brown sugar

Serves 4 to 6

sweet potato soup with chanterelle mushrooms

Sauté the onion and green onions in the butter in a kettle. Add the stock and sweet potatoes and simmer for 30 minutes or until tender. Cool slightly. Purée through a sieve or in a food processor and return to the kettle. Stir in the half-and-half and seasonings. Sauté the mushrooms in the olive oil in a sauté pan for 3 minutes. Add the chives. Spoon the soup into serving bowls and place the mushrooms in the center.

1 onion, chopped
2 green onions, chopped
2 tablespoons butter, melted
4 cups chicken stock
3 sweet potatoes, peeled and cut into chunks
3 cups half-and-half
Pinch of cayenne pepper
Pinch of grated nutmeg
Salt and black pepper to taste
1/2 cup chanterelle mushrooms
1 teaspoon olive oil
2 teaspoons chopped fresh chives

Serves 4 to 6

Blue Ridge Dining Room

chef's table

Blue Ridge Dining Room

stone ground grits and shrimp

To prepare the grits, bring the milk and water to a boil in a heavy saucepan over medium heat. Add the grits and salt. Reduce the heat to low. Simmer for 30 minutes, stirring occasionally. Add the butter, cream and pepper and simmer for 5 minutes, stirring occasionally. Keep warm in a double boiler, stirring frequently to prevent sticking.

To prepare the shrimp, heat the oil in a skillet until hot. Add the shrimp and shallots and sauté for 3 minutes. Add the garlic and sauté for 1 minute. Add the coffee, thyme, butter and brown sugar and bring to a boil. Season with salt and pepper. Serve over the hot grits.

stone ground grits

2 cups milk

2 cups water

1 cup stone ground grits

1 teaspoon salt

1/4 cup (1/2 stick) unsalted butter

1 cup heavy cream

2 teaspoons freshly ground pepper

shrimp

2 tablespoons vegetable oil

1 1/2 pounds (21- to 25-count) shrimp, peeled and deveined

3 shallots, chopped

1 garlic clove, chopped

1 cup strong coffee

1/4 teaspoon dried thyme

2 tablespoons butter, cut into cubes

1/2 teaspoon brown sugar

Salt and freshly ground pepper

Serves 4 to 6

chef's table

Bouchon

Owner/Chef

Michel Baudouin

62 North Lexington Avenue
Asheville, North Carolina 28801
828-350-1140
www.ashevillebouchon.com
Hours: Monday – Saturday
opening at 5:00 p.m.
AIR member

Michel Baudouin, chef-owner of Bouchon, started life in a 200-year-old farmhouse in France's Rhône Valley. His affinity for fine food and wine comes naturally. His father, Emile, was their village's premier amateur winegrower. Mother Antonia's way with a roast duck had neighbors and friends "coincidentally" dropping by at dinnertime every Sunday.

Michel's successes in the restaurant business began more than twenty years ago in the Dallas-Fort Worth area. His previous ventures include Michel Restaurant (cited by *Esquire* magazine as one of the nation's top fifty restaurants), Le Chardonnay (recognized by *Gourmet* and *Wine Spectator* magazines, in addition to many local honors), and Encore (named a "Best New" restaurant by *D* magazine).

Michel and his family (wife, Vonciel; daughter, Fuller; and cocker spaniel, Kappy) moved to Asheville after falling in love with the city on a visit.

poached pear in blue

To prepare the pears, peel the pears and place in a saucepan. Cover with the wine and add the peppercorns, juniper berries and bay leaf. Cook for 30 to 45 minutes, depending on the ripeness of the pears. (Keep the pears "al dente" so they will hold their shape and texture.) Remove the pears with a slotted spoon to a plate and let stand until cool to the touch. Cut the pears into halves lengthwise and remove the seeds with a melon baller. Fill the cavities of each pear half with blue cheese, reserving the remaining blue cheese for the salad. (The pears may be prepared the day before and stored in the refrigerator. Remove from the refrigerator 30 minutes before serving.)

To prepare the dressing, whisk the oil, balsamic vinegar, salt and pepper in a mixing bowl. Add the water gradually, whisking vigorously to emulsify. Whisk in the chives.

To prepare the salad, preheat the broiler. Place the pears on a baking sheet and broil until the cheese is light golden brown. Arrange 6 to 8 arugula leaves on each serving plate. Sprinkle with the pecans and reserved blue cheese. Drizzle with the dressing. Place a pear in the middle of each plate and serve immediately.

Bouchon

poached pears

2 pears, firm but not bruised
1 bottle red wine
6 whole peppercorns
6 whole juniper berries
1 bay leaf
8 ounces blue cheese, crumbled

chive dressing

2 tablespoons walnut oil
1 teaspoon balsamic vinegar
Salt and pepper to taste
1 tablespoon water
2 tablespoons chopped chives

salad

24 to 32 arugula leaves
1/2 cup roasted pecans

Serves 4

chef's table

mountain flavors

Bouchon

the field and stream

Prepare enough beans to serve four using the package directions and adding the lemon and 6 or 7 thyme sprigs. Chill, covered, for 8 to 10 hours. Whisk the cheese, sour cream, lemon juice, chopped chives, salt and pepper in a bowl until blended. Place in a pastry bag fitted with a filling tip and chill.

Sprinkle the fish with salt and pepper. Shape into a cornucopia (cone-like object) with the skin on the outside, securing with a wooden pick if needed. Place in a greased baking dish and fill each with the cheese mixture. Cover with plastic wrap and chill until ready to bake.

Preheat the oven to 400 degrees. Discard the thyme sprigs and lemon from the beans. Reheat the beans in a saucepan over low to medium heat, stirring frequently. Uncover the fish and add the wine. Bake for 12 to 15 minutes or until the fish flakes easily. Stir the spinach into the beans and cook until wilted. Spoon enough beans on the bottom of each plate to cover entirely. Place a cornucopia in the center of each plate using a flexible spatula and top with a generous amount of caviar. Garnish with additional sprigs of thyme or uncut chives. Serve immediately.

Bouchon

Great Northern beans, yellow eye beans, black beans, lima beans, or fava beans
1 lemon, cut into quarters
6 or 7 sprigs of fresh thyme
6 ounces fresh goat cheese, crumbled
6 tablespoons sour cream
Juice of 1 lemon
6 ounces chopped fresh chives
Salt and pepper to taste
4 trout fillets
1/3 cup white wine
4 cups fresh baby spinach
Trout caviar
Sprigs of thyme or uncut chives for garnish

Serves 4

chef's table
mountain flavors

Burgermeister's Kitchen and Tap

Owner/Chef

Tom Gaddy

697A Haywood Road
Asheville, North Carolina 28806
828-225-2920
www.burgermeisters.com
Hours: Closed Tuesday;
Lunch and Dinner
11:30 a.m. – 11:00 p.m.
Sunday –Thursday;
Friday and Saturday
11:30 a.m. – 1:00 a.m.
AIR member

Burgermeister's was founded on the idea of fun-filled, relaxed dining using fresh, high-quality ingredients.

The focus is on a wide variety of American classics with a vision for flavor, including gourmet burgers, hearty sandwiches, made-to-order salads, and tender seafood. The chef's specials are always a treat. Add a full bar, savory appetizers, or carnal desserts, and your experience is complete. The casual atmosphere serves as a backdrop to the great food and fun experience. Located in the heart of the old business district in West Asheville, it's a great place to meet friends, make friends, and break away from the rest of the world while refilling bellies and spirits.

The restaurant strives to make healthy food into comfort food. Portions are large, so sharing is encouraged—or stretch your dining dollar by taking half home for later.

fried pickle chips

Preheat the oil in a large stockpot to 375 degrees. Mix the flour, kosher salt, pepper, thyme, garlic powder and paprika in a bowl. Whisk the eggs and water in a bowl. Drain the pickle chips, discarding the brine. Dunk handfuls of the pickle chips at a time into the egg mixture and then remove and coat each pickle chip with the flour mixture, shaking off the excess. Add the coated pickle chips to the hot oil and deep-fry until golden brown. Serve immediately.

1 quart vegetable oil
2 cups all-purpose flour
2 teaspoons kosher salt
1 teaspoon pepper
1 teaspoon dried thyme
1 teaspoon garlic powder
1 teaspoon paprika
2 eggs
1/2 cup water
1 (16-ounce) jar thick sliced
    dill pickle chips

Serves 2 to 3 as an appetizer

Burgermeister's Kitchen and Tap

Whether you are new here or a regular local, here are great places to visit: Biltmore, The Blue Ridge Parkway, Great Smoky Mountains National Park, Cradle of Forestry, Grandfather Mountain, Connemara, Cherokee, Mount Mitchell State Park, North Carolina Arboretum, and Wheels Through Time Museum.

—Dale Neal, Asheville Citizen-Times

chef's table

Burgermeister's Kitchen and Tap

feta-sesame burger

Preheat the grill. Combine the ground beef, Worcestershire sauce and beer in a bowl and mix until combined. Mix the cheese, garlic, celery seeds, cilantro and sesame oil in a bowl, keeping the cheese chunky. Fold into the ground beef mixture. Divide into six equal portions. Shape each portion into a patty larger than the size of the bun to allow for shrinkage during grilling. Place on a grill rack and grill over medium-high heat for 4 minutes. Turn the patties and grill until cooked through. Place one patty on the bottom half of each bun. Top with leaf lettuce, tomato slices or any other toppings of choice. Top with the remaining half of the bun.

Burgermeister's Kitchen and Tap

2 pounds ground beef
1/3 cup Worcestershire sauce
1/2 cup beer (use your favorite)
3 ounces feta cheese, crumbled
1 garlic clove, minced
1/2 teaspoon celery seeds
2 teaspoons cilantro
2 teaspoons toasted sesame oil
6 hearty buns
Leaf lettuce, tomato slices or
    any other assorted toppings
    of choice

Serves 6

chef's table
mountain flavors

Café Azalea

Owners

*Judd and
Mackensy Lohof*

*1011 Tunnel Road
Asheville, North Carolina 28805
828-299-3753
Hours: Closed on Monday;
Tuesday – Friday
7:00 a.m. – 9:30 p.m.;
Saturday 8:00 a.m. – 9:30 p.m.;
Sunday 8:00 a.m. – 3:00 p.m.*

When you're in the mood for good times and great cuisine, be sure to check out Café Azalea. The restaurant is in one of the area's most pleasant settings and is known for its delightful staff and superb cuisine.

Café Azalea's menu follows an eclectic style it calls "healthy hedonism." Pleasurable recipes use wholesome ingredients like organic milk, free-range eggs, and local farm fresh vegetables. The chefs like good fats, like the omega-3 rich fish oil in the smoked salmon salad and olive oil in lieu of mayonnaise in the slaw. They also have a place in their hearts for bacon and butter—they are only human, and hedonists at that.

The chefs feel that food is a source of pleasure and should be regarded as such. They also believe that healthful foods need not to be austere. It's all about balance.

azalea mimosa

This is an easy but creative drink for a lazy summer brunch on the porch. We find that using nectars (easily found in either health food stores or Latino markets) gives the drink a better consistency than plain juice. We use a variety of pink nectars (the color is what makes it an Azalea Mimosa!), but we think that guava makes the best mimosas.

Peel the ginger. (Using a spoon works well for this.) Crush the root with the side of the blade of a chef's knife and chop into small pieces. Place the nectar, mint and chopped ginger in a pitcher and muddle gently with a wooden spoon. Let steep for 1 hour or longer for a stronger ginger-mint flavor. Strain the mixture into a pitcher, discarding the solids. Add the sparkling wine. Pour into Champagne flutes. Repeat as necessary until appropriately relaxed and lazy.

Note: Muddle means to mash or crush ingredients with a spoon to release the oils and flavors into the beverage.

1 (2-inch) piece fresh ginger
1 quart guava nectar
1/2 cup packed mint leaves
1 quart sparkling white wine
  (we like Kenwood Yalupa Brut)

Serves 4 to 6

Café Azalea

chef's table

mountain flavors

Café Azalea

lobster and butternut soup

Sweat the onion, fennel and celery in the oil in a large saucepan over medium-high heat until soft and translucent, making sure not to brown. Remove from the heat. Add the brandy, stirring to deglaze the saucepan. Return to the heat and stir. Reduce the heat to low. Add the tomato purée and cook for a few minutes. Add the half-and-half, stock and squash and simmer until the squash softens. Add the parsley, chives, tarragon, lobster meat, salt and pepper and simmer just until the lobster meat is heated through. Ladle into soup bowls.

Café Azalea

1 yellow onion, chopped
1/2 fennel bulb, chopped
2 ribs celery, chopped
2 tablespoons vegetable oil
Splash of brandy
1/4 cup tomato purée
1 quart half-and-half
1 quart lobster stock
    (lobster base mixed with
    water works fine)
1 cup chopped peeled
    butternut squash
2 tablespoons minced parsley
1 tablespoon minced chives
1 1/2 teaspoons minced tarragon
8 ounces lobster meat, cooked
Salt and pepper to taste

Serves 8 to 10

chef's table

mountain flavors

Café on the Square

Executive Chef

Wilson Hawes

One Biltmore Avenue
Asheville, North Carolina 28801
828-251-5565
www.cafeonthesquare.com
Hours: Lunch: Monday – Saturday
11:30 a.m. – 3:00 p.m.;
Dinner: Monday – Thursday
5:00 p.m. – 9:00 p.m.,
Friday and Saturday
5:00 p.m. – 10:00 p.m.
Sunday is seasonal 5:00 p.m. – 9:00 p.m.
On- and off-site catering is available;
please call for information.
AIR member

Owner Tracy Adler settled in Asheville in 1999. A plastics program manager by trade, she is the managing partner of Café on the Square. Chef Wilson Hawes came to the food business as countless others do—as a musician trying to make ends meet. Tracy gives Wilson free reign over his staff, the menus, and his schedule, which includes weekly gigs with his band, East Coast Dirt.

Located at the center of Asheville's beautiful downtown district, Café on the Square is ideal for lunch and fine evening dining. Large picture windows enable diners to watch the hustle and bustle of Pack Square while enjoying fine American cuisine. Seasonal menus offer a variety of choice-cut meats, pasta, seafood, and vegetarian dishes. Whether you're planning a day in the art galleries, an evening at the Diana Wortham Theater, or just finishing a day on the golf course, you'll be pleased with the elegant yet comfortable atmosphere of Café on the Square.

chargrilled black angus bistro tenderloin

To prepare the port diviande, bring the wine, thyme, peppercorns, bay leaves, garlic and shallots to a boil in a 1-quart saucepan. Cook until the volume is reduced by one-half. Add the demi-glace and cook until the sauce is reduced and coats the back of a spoon. Strain the sauce, discarding the solids. Season with salt and pepper. Whisk in the cold butter.

To prepare the grits, bring the water, cream and butter to a boil in a saucepan. Stir in the grits. Reduce the heat and simmer for 30 minutes, stirring occasionally. Stir in the cheese and lemon juice. Season with salt and pepper.

To assemble, cut the beef into slices and serve over the grits and vegetable of choice. Finish with the port diviande.

Note: Demi-glace is a rich espagnole sauce made with slowly cooked beef stock and sherry that has been cooked until reduced by one-half.

port diviande
8 ounces port

4 sprigs of thyme

1 tablespoon black peppercorns

3 bay leaves

3 garlic cloves

2 shallots, coarsely chopped

2 ounces demi-glace or reduced
    beef stock

Salt and pepper to taste

1/2 tablespoon butter

gorgonzola grits
4 cups water

4 cups cream

1/4 cup (1/2 stick) butter

2 cups stone ground grits

1 cup (4 ounces) shredded
    gorgonzola cheese

Splash of fresh lemon juice

Salt and pepper to taste

assembly
1 (3- to 4-pound) Black Angus
    beef tenderloin, grilled

Vegetable of choice

Serves 8

Café on the Square

chef's table
mountain flavors

chef's table

mountain flavors

Café on the Square

cajun fried eggplant

Dip the eggplant in lightly beaten eggs and cover with a mixture of bread crumbs and 1 teaspoon Cajun seasoning to coat. Heat the olive oil in a skillet. Add the eggplant and fry until golden brown.

Season the shrimp, crawfish, scallops and sausage with 1 teaspoon Cajun seasoning. Sauté with the garlic, bell pepper, onion and mushrooms in olive oil in a large skillet. Season with salt and pepper. Add the Tabasco sauce and tarragon. Add the sherry, stirring to deglaze the skillet. Add the cream and butter and cook until the sauce is reduced and thick. Serve with the eggplant.

Note: Chicken also can be used in addition to or instead of the seafood.

2 (1/4-inch-thick) slices
  peeled eggplant
Eggs, lightly beaten
Bread crumbs
1 teaspoon Cajun seasoning
Olive oil for frying
3 shrimp
1 ounce crawfish meat
3 scallops
1 ounce andouille
1 teaspoon Cajun seasoning
1 teaspoon fresh garlic
1 ounce bell pepper
1 ounce red onion
1 ounce portobello mushrooms
Olive oil for sautéing
Salt and pepper to taste
1 teaspoon Tabasco sauce
1 teaspoon fresh tarragon
1/4 cup cooking sherry
2 tablespoons heavy cream
1 tablespoon butter

Serves 1

chef's table

mountain flavors

Charlotte Street Grill and Pub

Chef

Tyler Cook

157 Charlotte Street
Asheville, North Carolina 28801
828-253-5348
www.charlottestreetgrill.com
Hours: Monday – Friday
11:30 a.m. – 2:00 p.m.;
Monday – Thursday
5:00 p.m. – 9:00 p.m.;
Friday and Saturday
5:00 p.m. – 2:30 a.m.
AIR member

Today, guests from this area and around the world agree that Charlotte Street Grill and Pub has evolved to satisfy even the most selective palate.

Come experience the casual elegance of dining in the charming Victorian rooms upstairs. The plentiful grill-style menu and affordable prices will delight your senses and sensibility.

Enjoy the festive and intimate "European Public House" atmosphere in The Pub downstairs. For a bounty of light fare in a lively atmosphere, visit The Pub. Whatever your tastes, you can enjoy an extensive array of mixed drinks and more than two dozen local beers and wines from the full bar.

For a unique and intimate dining experience, an accommodating atmosphere for groups, or a great place to just get away for a while, come to the Charlotte Street Grill and Pub.

broiled trout with green tomato marmalade

To prepare the grits, bring the water, wine and cream to a boil in a saucepan. Whisk in the grits, salt and pepper. Cook over low heat for 25 to 30 minutes or until thickened, stirring frequently. Stir in the butter. Pour into a greased flat-bottomed dish. Cool and chill.

To prepare the marmalade, mix the tomatoes, lemon juice, sugar and salt in a bowl. Let stand for 1 hour. Place in a non-reactive saucepan and simmer for 1 hour or until the tomatoes are soft and the liquid is reduced and amber colored. Cool and then chill.

To prepare the trout and assemble, preheat the broiler. Season the trout with salt and pepper and coat liberally with the marmalade. Place on a rack in a broiler pan and broil at medium temperature for 5 to 7 minutes or until the marmalade begins to caramelize. Cut the grits into desired shapes and season with salt and pepper. Dip in buttermilk and dredge in flour. Fry in half the oil in a small sauté pan until brown and crisp. Season the green beans with salt and pepper. Dip in buttermilk. Dredge in flour and then cornmeal. Fry in the remaining oil in a small sauté pan until brown and crispy. Plate the fried grits and fried green beans with the trout. Garnish with the parsley.

Charlotte Street Grill and Pub

grits
3 cups water
1/4 cup white wine
1 cup heavy cream
1 cup white grits
Salt and pepper to taste
1/4 cup (1/2 stick) butter

green tomato marmalade
4 large green tomatoes, chopped
Juice of 4 lemons
1 cup sugar
1 tablespoon salt

broiled trout and assembly
4 (8-ounce) boneless trout fillets
Salt and pepper to taste
Buttermilk, all-purpose flour and
    cornmeal for dredging
1/2 cup vegetable oil
1 pound fresh green beans,
    trimmed and snapped
2 tablespoons chopped parsley
    for garnish

Serves 4

chef's table

mountain flavors

Charlotte Street Grill and Pub

parchment roasted chicken

Preheat the oven to 450 degrees. Season the chicken with salt, pepper and the lemon zest. Use a small amount of the butter to coat four 12×15-inch sheets of baking parchment and sprinkle with the parsley. Arrange two lemon slices in the center of each sheet and top with the leeks. Arrange three artichoke halves on each side of the lemon slices and leeks for a total of six per package. Place the chicken on top. Sprinkle with the tomatoes and season with salt and pepper. Fold each baking parchment by its length and width to form a tight package, enclosing the ingredients. Place the packages lemon side up on a lightly greased baking sheet. Roast for 7 to 10 minutes or until a meat thermometer inserted into the middle of the package registers 190 degrees.

Divide the remaining butter into four equal portions and sprinkle with the tarragon.

Serve by opening the baking parchment packages with a pair of scissors and topping with the tarragon butter. Serve with steamed rice or roasted potatoes.

4 (6-ounce) chicken breasts
Salt and pepper to taste
1 teaspoon lemon zest
1/2 cup (1 stick) butter
1 tablespoon chopped parsley
8 thin lemon slices
White portion of 2 leeks,
  julienned
12 whole canned artichokes,
  cut into halves
2 beefsteak tomatoes,
  coarsely chopped
1 tablespoon chopped tarragon

Serves 4

Charlotte Street Grill and Pub

chef's table

mountain flavors

Chef in Motion

Chef

Mauricio Abreu

57 Victoria Road
Asheville, North Carolina 28801
828-350-8999
www.chefinmotion.com
Hours: Monday – Friday
8:00 a.m. – 5:00 p.m.;
Dinner by reservation
Monday – Saturday
AIR member

Chef Mo and Brenda pride themselves on serving delicious, carefully crafted food in warm surroundings. They translate their mid-Western roots to give new meaning to home-style and comfort food in this one-of-a-kind restaurant.

The lunch menu offers homemade soups, sandwiches featuring Mo's focaccia, salads with "Mo-made" dressings, and other specialties you'll need to taste. Everyone loves the homemade Oreos.

Treat yourself to a unique new experience for dinner. Courses are designed especially for you at affordable prices. Create your menu with Chef Mo or leave it all up to him. Attention to your personal culinary preferences will set this dining affair apart. You also can turn your dinner into a cooking class party with Chef Mo in our open kitchen!

"No rush . . . . No distractions . . . . . .
Our house is your house . . . . for the night!"

chef mo's duck mole negro

To prepare the mole negro, roast the chiles in an open fire or in a cast-iron skillet, being careful not to burn. Remove the seeds and set the chiles aside. Bring 1/3 cup olive oil to the smoke state in a large skillet. Sauté the chiles, onions, tomatoes, romaine, tortillas, garlic, cilantro, oregano and cumin in small batches in the hot olive oil, being careful not to burn the garlic and adding additional olive oil as needed. Add the stock, chocolate and cinnamon stick. Cook for 10 to 15 minutes over medium heat. Add the salt and pepper and let cool. Discard the cinnamon stick and blend together. Strain and scrape into a bowl with a wire whisk. (This will make 1 quart. May add additional stock if needed. The paste can be chilled in an airtight container for up to 2 weeks. It also can be frozen. Reconstitute to the desired consistency with additional stock and season with salt and pepper to taste.)

To prepare the duck and assemble, preheat the oven to 350 degrees. Sauté the duck skin side down in the olive oil in a hot ovenproof sauté pan for 5 minutes. Turn and sauté for 3 minutes. Season with salt and pepper and bake until the duck is cooked through. Let stand for a couple of minutes before serving. Serve the mole under and over the duck breast. Great served with rice or roasted vegetables.

mole negro

8 ounces dried guajillo chiles
8 ounces dried ancho chiles
8 ounces dried New Mexican chiles
8 ounces dried chipotle chiles
8 ounces mulato or cascabel chiles
1/3 cup olive oil
1 1/2 red onions, coarsely chopped
4 tomatoes, chopped
1/2 heart of romaine, chopped
4 corn tortillas, chopped
8 garlic cloves
1/2 bunch cilantro
1 tablespoon dried oregano
1 tablespoon cumin
1 quart chicken or vegetable stock
1 bar Mexican chocolate
    (Abuelita), coarsely chopped
1 cinnamon stick
1 teaspoon salt
1 teaspoon pepper

sautéed duck and assembly

Duck breast
1 tablespoon olive oil
Salt and pepper to taste

Serves 2

chef's table
mountain flavors

Chef in Motion

ceviche

Cut the fish into small pieces and place in a bowl. Add the lime juice. Marinate in the refrigerator for 2 hours or longer. (The longer the better.) Add the olive oil, onion, tomatoes, cilantro, chile and olives and stir to mix. Season with salt and pepper. Chill until ready to serve. To serve, spoon the fish mixture into margarita glasses rimmed with salt. Cut the avocado into halves and remove the seed. Remove from the skin and cut into slices. Place on top of the fish mixture. Garnish with lime slices and serve with crostini.

2 pounds fresh fish such as swordfish, mahi-mahi, corvina, halibut or sea bass (sushi grade if available), or shellfish such as shrimp, lobster or scallops
Juice of 4 to 6 limes
1/4 cup extra-virgin olive oil
1 red onion, finely chopped
2 tomatoes, finely chopped
1/4 bunch cilantro, chopped
1 jalapeño chile, finely chopped
1/4 cup green olives, chopped
Salt and pepper to taste
1 avocado
Lime slices for garnish

Serves 6

Chef in Motion

chef's table

Chelsea's

Proprietor

Cindy Piercy

Six Boston Way
Historic Biltmore Village
Asheville, North Carolina 28803
828-274-4400
www.chelseastea.com
Hours: Lunch 11:30 a.m. – 3:00 p.m.;
proper English Afternoon Tea
at 3:30 p.m. Monday – Saturday;
Sunday Brunch 10:30 a.m. – 3:00 p.m.
April – December
AIR member

Each afternoon at Chelsea's recreates the sense of a bygone era through the charm and elegance of its setting in a little cottage. You're invited to "Take Tea" with the family. Choose the Tea Plate with an amazing selection of sweets and savories or the cheese board with a selection of cheeses, grilled bread, and fresh fruit. You may choose from Elmwood Inn Fine Teas or from an array of other black and herb teas. Many of the teas, desserts, and other tea items can be purchased in the gift shop to enjoy at home.

Chelsea's offers a world of contentment. Surround yourself with French and English antiques, as well as very special imported items. Each item has been chosen for its beauty and originality.

chelsea's classic pasta salad

Cook the pasta in boiling water in a saucepan until tender. Drain and rinse with cold water. Combine the pasta, celery, onion and peas in a large bowl and toss to mix. Combine the dill weed, dressing mix, lemon juice, buttermilk, mayonnaise and sour cream in a large mixing bowl and mix well. Season with salt and pepper. Add to the pasta mixture and stir gently to coat. Chill for 2 hours or until serving time.

1 pound rotini
4 ribs celery, finely chopped
1 red onion, finely chopped
1 cup frozen peas, thawed
2 tablespoons chopped fresh dill
    weed, or 1 tablespoon dried
    dill weed
1 envelope ranch salad
    dressing mix
Juice of 1/2 lemon
2 tablespoons buttermilk
1/2 cup mayonnaise
1/2 cup sour cream
Salt and pepper to taste

Serves 8

It is an artist's abode in the mountains. Seasonal gallery walks are held in Asheville, as well as Hendersonville, Waynesville, and Brevard.
                                    —*Paul Clark*, Asheville Citizen-Times

chef's table

Chelsea's

70

chelsea's chicken salad

Cook the chicken in boiling water in a large saucepan until tender. Remove from the heat and rinse with cool water. Cut the chicken into 1/2-inch cubes. Combine the chicken, celery and onion in a medium mixing bowl and mix well. Chill, covered, in the refrigerator. Combine the yogurt, mayonnaise, sour cream and lemon juice in a small bowl and mix well. Add to the chicken mixture and mix well.

6 boneless skinless
chicken breasts
1/2 cup chopped celery
1/2 cup chopped red onion
1/4 cup plain yogurt
1/4 cup mayonnaise
1/4 cup sour cream
Juice of 1/2 lemon

Serves 6 to 8

Variations:

To prepare Tarragon Chicken Salad, add 1/2 cup halved seedless grapes and 1/2 cup chopped walnuts to the salad. Add 1 tablespoon dried tarragon (or 2 tablespoons chopped fresh tarragon) and 1 teaspoon horseradish to the dressing.

To prepare Curried Chicken Salad, add 1/2 bunch green onions, chopped, to the salad. Add 2 teaspoons curry powder, 1 tablespoon chopped fresh cilantro and 1/4 cup fruit chutney to the dressing.

To prepare Chicken Club Salad, add 1/2 cup crumbled cooked bacon, 1/2 cup diced ham and 1 cup quartered cherry tomatoes to the salad. Add 2 tablespoons whole grain mustard to the dressing.

City Bakery Café

Owner

Brendan Dennehy

60 Biltmore Avenue
Asheville, North Carolina 28801
828-252-4426
www.citybakery.net
Hours: Monday – Thursday
7:00 a.m. – 7:00 p.m.;
Friday – Saturday 7:00 a.m. – 9:00 p.m.;
Sunday 8:00 a.m. – 5:00 p.m.
88 Charlotte Street
Asheville, North Carolina 28801
828-254-4289
Hours: Monday – Friday
7:00 a.m. – 6:00 p.m.;
Saturday 7:00 a.m. – 4:00 p.m.
AIR member

City Bakery is a family-owned and -operated bakery with two locations in beautiful Asheville, specializing in scratch-made artisan breads, cakes, and pastries.

The bakery takes pride in delightful lunch and dinner offerings, featuring panini and deli-style sandwiches, scratch-made soups, and refreshing salads incorporating fresh-baked artisan breads with the highest quality ingredients.

City Bakery also offers a huge array of scratch-made cakes for every occasion. From birthday cakes to wedding cakes—and everything in between—the custom cakes are sure to be a big hit at your next event.

City Bakery's goal has been to provide Asheville and its surrounding communities with fresh-baked, quality products. It is committed to using only the highest-quality, all-natural ingredients and organic flours.

Visit one of the cafés to enjoy quality baked goods and meals in a relaxed atmosphere with great service.

farmhouse oatmeal bread

To prepare the poolish or starter, combine the water, yeast, bread flour and wheat flour in a mixing bowl. Mix with a spoon or at low speed with an electric mixer for 5 minutes. Cover and chill for 8 to 10 hours.

To prepare the soaker, combine the water, oats and molasses in a bowl. Let stand for 2 hours prior to mixing the dough.

To prepare the bread, mix the bread flour, yeast and sea salt together in a large mixing bowl. Add the poolish and soaker and mix well with a spoon or with your hands until all of the ingredients are mixed together. (The dough should have a slightly sticky consistency.) Cover with a dishcloth and let rise for 1 hour. (The dough should rise slightly.) Punch and fold the dough to strengthen the gluten and let stand for 1 hour.

Preheat the oven to 450 degrees. Place the dough on a lightly floured surface. Divide the dough into four equal portions. Shape each portion into a loaf, making sure all air pockets are eliminated. Place on a baking sheet lined with baking parchment. Spray the top of the loaves with water and sprinkle with rolled oats. Let stand for 30 minutes. Bake for 20 to 25 minutes or until the loaves test done, checking the bread after 15 minutes. Remove to wire racks to cool.

poolish
1¹/4 pounds water
.05 ounce instant dry yeast
8 ounces bread flour
8 ounces wheat flour

soaker
.5625 pound water
.4375 pound rolled oats
.1875 pound molasses

bread
1.125 pounds bread flour
.15 ounce instant dry yeast
.825 ounce sea salt
Rolled oats for sprinkling

Makes 4 loaves

City Bakery Café

peanut butter brownie cheesecake

To prepare the brownie layer, preheat the oven to 375 degrees. Grease a 9-inch springform pan well and line the bottom with baking parchment. Melt the chocolate in a double boiler over hot water and set aside. Cream the butter and sugar in a mixing bowl until light and fluffy. Add the eggs and vanilla and mix well. Beat in the melted chocolate. Add the flour and salt and mix well. Pour into the prepared pan and bake for 30 minutes or until a wooden pick inserted in the center comes out clean. Remove from the oven.

To prepare the cheesecake layer, reduce the oven temperature to 325 degrees. Beat the cream cheese and peanut butter in a mixing bowl until smooth, scraping the side of the bowl frequently. Add the sugar and beat until fluffy. Add the flour and mix well. Add the eggs and vanilla gradually, beating constantly until smooth; do not overmix. Pour over the brownie layer. Bake for 45 to 60 minutes or until the middle springs back when lightly touched. Chill in the refrigerator for 8 to 10 hours before cutting.

City Bakery Café

brownie layer

$4^{1}/_{2}$ ounces unsweetened chocolate
1 cup (2 sticks) unsalted butter, softened
$1^{1}/_{2}$ cups sugar
3 eggs
$1^{1}/_{2}$ teaspoons vanilla extract
$1^{1}/_{2}$ cups all-purpose flour
$^{3}/_{4}$ teaspoon salt

cheesecake layer

24 ounces cream cheese, softened
8 ounces creamy peanut butter
1 cup sugar
2 teaspoons all-purpose flour
3 eggs
$1^{1}/_{2}$ teaspoons vanilla extract

Serves 12

chef's table

Corner Kitchen

Owner

Joe Scully

3 Boston Way
Asheville, North Carolina 28803
828-274-2439
www.thecornerkitchen.com
Hours: Breakfast, Lunch, and Dinner
7 days a week
AIR member

The Corner Kitchen's style of cuisine is best described as American Bistro fare with a definite Southern slant.

Its approach is as unassuming as its name. Owners Kevin Westmoreland and Joe Scully allow most things to speak for themselves and word-of-mouth to be their principal marketing tool. While there are other places in Asheville to get great food, there is no other setting where a guest can get the culinary, architectural, and service experience The Corner Kitchen provides.

Kevin and Joe extend their personal commitment to quality by offering guests the finest in service, ambiance, food, and value. They employ the best and most service-oriented staff, buy the best possible food, and apply Joe's impressive experience and skills to menu development and food preparation.

The Corner Kitchen is in historic Biltmore Village.

summer melon yin/yang soup with ginger

Purée the cantaloupe, cream to taste and salt in a food processor. Add lemon juice and mix well. Pour into a pitcher. Purée the honeydew melon, cream to taste and salt in a food processor. Add lime juice and mix well. Pour into a pitcher. Purée the ginger in a food processor. Strain the ginger, reserving the ginger juice and discarding the solids. Whip 1/2 cup whipping cream and the reserved ginger juice in a mixing bowl until soft peaks form. Pour the cantaloupe mixture and honeydew mixture simultaneously into serving bowls. Add a dollop of the ginger cream and a little basil.

*1 cantaloupe, peeled, seeded
    and cubed*
Heavy cream to taste
Salt to taste
Lemon juice to taste
*1 honeydew melon, peeled, seeded
    and cubed*
Lime juice to taste
2 tablespoons fresh ginger
1/2 cup heavy whipping cream
*1 tablespoon thin slivers
    Thai basil*

Serves 8

Corner Kitchen

josh week's famous bread pudding

Preheat the oven to 350 degrees. Cut the bread into 1/2-inch cubes and toss with the butter to coat. Spread on a baking sheet and bake until toasted a light golden brown. Mix the milk, sugar, cinnamon and vanilla in a saucepan and heat until scalded. Beat the eggs in a mixing bowl. Add a small amount of the scalded mixture to the beaten eggs. Whisk the eggs into the scalded mixture. Add the white chocolate and whisk until melted. Strain the custard.

Butter 8-ounce soufflé molds and place 1/2 to 3/4 cup toasted bread cubes into each. Pour 1/2 cup custard over each. Bake for 25 minutes or until golden brown and the custard is cooked through.

Corner Kitchen

1 loaf white bread
1/2 cup (1 stick) butter, melted
4 cups milk
2 cups sugar
1 tablespoon cinnamon
1 teaspoon vanilla extract
12 eggs
1 cup grated white chocolate

Serves 12

chef's table

ED Boudreaux's

Co-owners

*Dustin Vanderbunt and
Eric Feichter*

*48 Biltmore Avenue
Asheville, North Carolina 28801
828-296-0100
Hours: 11:30 a.m. – 11:00 p.m.
BAR OPEN LATE
AIR member*

ED Boudreaux's Bayou Bar-B-Que serves fresh food at affordable prices, as well as amazing barbecue. Whether you choose pork, beef, chicken, or ribs, there are fourteen in-house sauces to complement them all. With names like Voodoo, Memphis Red, Alabama White, Mississippi Mud, or ED's Original Creole, hot is the word of the day. ED Boudreaux's sauces are so popular, they now have them bottled and for sale in the restaurant and on the Web site.

If meat's not your thing, there's a large vegetarian menu with tempting dishes such as the Artichoke and Spinach Melt, the Tempeh Reuben, or the popular Avocado Melt.

Whether meat or vegetarian, the fifteen side dishes made fresh daily offer a complement sure to please everyone.

To quench your thirst, choose from over 140 different beers in stock and the extensive wine list.

ED's features live music five nights a week with no cover and a full bar.

backwoods barbecue sauce and mop

Combine the vinegar, onions, ketchup, mustard, Worcestershire sauce, brown sugar and pepper in a saucepan and mix well. Bring to a boil and reduce the heat. Simmer for 20 minutes, thinning with beer if the sauce becomes too thick.

2 cups apple cider vinegar
2 Vidalia onions, finely chopped
2 cups ketchup
1/2 cup yellow mustard
1/2 cup Worcestershire sauce
1 cup packed brown sugar
2 tablespoons pepper
1 can beer (if needed)

Makes 6 cups

ed's original baked pasta with vermont cheddar

Preheat the oven to 350 degrees. Whisk the flour in the butter in a saucepan over medium-high heat for 2 minutes or until pale yellow. Whisk in the milk gradually. Cook for 3 to 5 minutes or until thickened, stirring constantly. Add the salt and pepper. Simmer for 3 to 5 minutes, stirring constantly. Whisk in the cheese until melted. (Add a little milk if needed.) Remove from the heat. Fold in the egg yolks and adjust the seasonings. Add the pasta and spoon into a buttered baking dish. Bake, covered, for 45 minutes. Bake, uncovered, until light brown. Cool for 15 minutes before serving.

1/2 cup all-purpose flour
1/2 cup (1 stick) butter, melted
2 quarts milk, warmed
1 teaspoon salt
1/2 teaspoon white pepper
1 pound Vermont sharp white
    Cheddar cheese, shredded
8 egg yolks
2 pounds ziti or mini
    penne, cooked

Serves 8

ED Boudreaux's

chef's table **81**
mountain flavors

chef's table

mountain flavors

ED Boudreaux's

white chocolate cranberry bread pudding with amaretto sauce

To prepare the bread pudding, preheat the oven to 375 degrees. Soak the cranberries in the amaretto to plump. Combine the eggs, cream and vanilla in a bowl and mix well. Add the bread and stir to coat. Let stand for 30 minutes for the bread to absorb the cream mixture. Fold in the almonds, undrained cranberries and white chocolate chips. Spoon into a baking dish. Cover and place in a larger baking dish. Add enough water to the larger baking dish to come halfway up the side of the smaller baking dish. Bake for 1 hour or until firm. (Do not use a convection oven.)

To prepare the sauce, heat the sugar and water in a saucepan until the mixture is golden brown. Remove from the heat. Stir in the amaretto and cream. Let cool to room temperature.

To serve, cut the bread pudding into small pieces because of the sweetness and serve with the sauce.

ED Boudreaux's

bread pudding
$1^1/2$ cups dried cranberries
$^1/2$ cup amaretto
8 eggs
1 quart heavy cream
1 tablespoon vanilla extract
2 loaves French bread, cubed and
    dried at room temperature
$1^1/2$ cups sliced almonds, toasted
2 cups (12 ounces) white
    chocolate chips

amaretto sauce
3 cups sugar
$^1/2$ cup water
$^1/2$ cup amaretto
1 quart heavy cream

Serves 16

chef's table

fig

Executive Chef

Bill Klein

18 Brook Street
Suite 101
Asheville, North Carolina 28803
828-277-0889
www.figbistro.com
Hours: Monday – Saturday:
Lunch 11:00 a.m. – 3:00 p.m.;
Dinner 5:30 p.m. – 9:00 p.m.
AIR member

Trace and Treavis Taylor created fig in Biltmore Village by assimilating the best of their own dining experiences from their travels throughout Europe and North America. Fig offers classic bistro cuisine in a comfortable, yet elegant, atmosphere.

Fig offers authentic bistro cuisine prepared with the freshest and finest ingredients available. Commitment to quality and excellence is readily apparent in the culinary masterpieces created by French-trained Chef William Klein. An exceptional wine list provides the perfect complement.

The cozy dining room is elegant, yet casual, with hardwood floors, sleek black chairs, and classic bistro tables creating a European/Cosmopolitan ambiance. Weather permitting, patrons can enjoy the serenity of dining in the quiet courtyard. Fig completes the experience with a professional and engaging staff. The ultimate goal is to create a memorable dining experience without pretension.

north carolina flounder

Sweat the shallots in canola oil in a skillet until tender. Add salt, lemon grass, 8 ounces carrots and lime leaves and juice in a juicer. Pour into a large saucepan. Add 2½ pounds carrots and the ginger and bring to a boil. Add the coconut milk and simmer until the carrots are tender. Purée in a blender and strain. Return to the saucepan. Stir in the fish sauce and let stand until cool. Finish the sauce with lime juice and julienned mint.

Season the cucumbers with salt. Strain in a strainer for 1 hour. Squeeze dry. Sauté in hot canola oil in a skillet. Add salt, the shrimp and stock and cook until the shrimp turn pink.

Season fish with salt and white pepper. Sear in a hot sauté pan until golden brown.

Place the shrimp mixture in the center of a heated bowl. Spoon 4 to 6 tablespoons of the hot carrot broth over the shrimp. (Thin the broth if needed. The consistency should be thicker than chicken noodle soup.) Top with the fish and garnish with fresh mint.

Note: There will be some of the carrot broth left over. Store in the refrigerator and use the next day to poach some shrimp.

5 shallots, minced
Canola oil for sweating
Salt to taste
5 lemon grass stalks,
  finely chopped
8 ounces carrots, coarsely chopped
4 kaffir lime leaves
2½ pounds carrots,
  coarsely chopped
1 ounce fresh ginger
2 cans coconut milk
1½ teaspoons fish sauce
Fresh lime juice
Julienned mint
2 cucumbers, cut on the bias and
  into half moon shapes
Canola oil for sautéing
1 cup rock shrimp, peeled and
  deveined (¼ cup per serving)
¾ cup chicken stock
4 (6-ounce) North Carolina
  flounder fillets
White pepper to taste
Fresh mint for garnish

Serves 4

fig

warm potato salad and caviar

Cut the potatoes into small pieces and rinse under cold water until the water runs clear. Place in a saucepan and cover with cold water and a generous pinch of salt. Bring to a boil and turn off the heat. Let stand just until the potatoes are tender. Drain and spread on a sheet tray to cool. (You may prepare one day ahead and chill. Bring to room temperature 1 hour before serving.)

Whisk the egg yolks, lemon juice, Dijon mustard, 1/4 teaspoon salt and the white pepper in a glass, ceramic or stainless steel bowl. Whisk in the grape seed oil one drop at a time until the mixture begins to thicken and stiffen. (All of the ingredients are to remain at room temperature.) Store in the refrigerator for one to two days.

Bring enough water to cover the potatoes to a boil in a saucepan. Remove from the heat and add the prepared potatoes. Let stand to reheat; drain. Mix the egg mixture with the vinegar and water to thin. Add to the potatoes and mix to coat. Add the chives and adjust the salt to taste. Warm spoons in hot water and set on paper towels. Place potato salad on each spoon and garnish with caviar. Or, you may mold the potato salad as shown at left and top with caviar.

2 medium to large Yukon
   Gold potatoes
Generous pinch of salt
2 pasteurized egg yolks
Juice of 1/2 lemon
1 1/2 teaspoons Dijon mustard
1/4 teaspoon salt
White pepper to taste
1 cup grape seed oil or canola oil
Shot of sherry vinegar
Shot of water
Finely chopped chives
Caviar for garnish

Serves 4

chef's table

mountain flavors

Fiore's

Owner/Chef

Anthony Cerrato

122 College Street
Asheville, North Carolina 28801
828-281-0710
Web: www.fioresasheville.com
Hours: Serving lunch
11:00 a.m. – 3:30 p.m.;
Dinner 4:30 p.m. – 10:00 p.m.
Monday – Saturday. Closed
on Sunday.
AIR member

Named after Chef Anthony Cerrato's grandfather, Fiore's showcases the elegance, tradition, and passion of many generations of great peasant cooks. The concept is based on principles that Chef Cerrato believes to be true: Great food takes great products, passion, and many years of training.

Fiore's is set in an elegantly restored (by his father's own hands) turn-of-the-century building, with brick walls and warm wooden booths that are enhanced by original works of local art.

Fiore's menu selections include old classics such as shrimp scampi and vitello marsala, as well as more innovative Tuscan-inspired cuisine such as rosemary grilled duck breast served with asiago and prosciutto-wrapped figs with aged balsamic vinegar.

Join Chef Cerrato for a relaxing evening of rustic Tuscan cuisine, handpicked Italian wines and old-world hospitality!

Bevenuti alla nostra casa e Buone Appetito!

rigatoni alla vodka

Cook the pasta using the package directions in a large saucepan until al dente. Drain the pasta and rinse well with warm water. Heat the butter and olive oil in a large skillet over medium-high to high heat. Add the garlic and sauté until soft and fragrant. (Do not brown.) Add the vodka and cook until the alcohol evaporates. Add 4 sprigs basil, 2 sprigs parsley, red pepper flakes, salt and black pepper. Reduce the heat to medium-high. Add the cream and mix well. Add the tomatoes and cook for 6 minutes. Add 1 cup cheese and stir to mix well. Add the pasta to the sauce and toss to coat. Place on serving plates and garnish with 1 tablespoon basil, 1 tablespoon parsley and 1 tablespoon cheese.

Fiore's

1 pound dry rigatoni (premium
   Italian brand)
1/2 cup (1 stick) unsalted butter
1/2 cup extra-virgin olive oil
1/4 cup coarsely chopped
   crushed garlic
6 ounces vodka
4 sprigs of fresh sweet basil,
   chiffinade
2 sprigs of flat Italian parsley,
   coarsely chopped
Red pepper flakes to taste
Salt and black pepper to taste
2 cups heavy cream
2 (16-ounce) cans crushed
   Italian tomatoes
1 cup (4 ounces) grated pecorino
   Romano cheese
1 tablespoon chiffinade basil
   for garnish
1 tablespoon chopped parsley
   for garnish
1 tablespoon grated Romano
   cheese for garnish

Serves 6 to 8

chef's table

mountain flavors

Fiore's

chianti-glazed bistecca

To prepare the beef, remove the sinew and excess fat from the beef. Rub with olive oil, sea salt and black pepper. Mix the wine, brown sugar, red pepper, black pepper, sea salt and rosemary in a small saucepan. Cook until the mixture is reduced by one-half. Discard the rosemary. Preheat the grill. Place the beef on a grill rack and grill to the desired degree of doneness. Glaze the beef with the sauce. Cut into slices and drizzle with the remaining sauce.

To prepare the figs, preheat the oven to 400 degrees. Remove the stems from the figs and slice to butterfly each. Add ¼ ounce cheese to the center of each fig and then close the fig. Wrap each fig with a large basil leaf and then wrap with a slice of the prosciutto, securing with a wooden pick. Place on a sizzle pan and drizzle with olive oil. Roast for 3 to 5 minutes. Serve as an accompaniment to the beef.

Fiore's

beef

2 pounds prime rib Black Angus
    beef tenderloin
Extra-virgin olive oil
Sea salt to taste
Cracked black pepper to taste
12 ounces chianti
1/3 cup packed brown sugar
Crushed red pepper to taste
Sprig of fresh rosemary

figs

12 dried Calimyrna or
    Adriatic figs
3 ounces goat cheese
12 fresh large basil leaves
12 (1×3-inch) pieces prosciutto
Extra-virgin olive oil
    for drizzling

Serves 4

chef's table

mountain flavors

Flying Frog

Owner/Chef

Vijay Shastri

1 Battery Park Avenue
Asheville, North Carolina 28801
828-254-9411
www.flyingfrogcafe.com
Hours: Sunday, Wednesday –
Thursday 5:30 p.m. – 9:30 p.m.;
Friday and Saturday
5:30 p.m. – 11:00 p.m.
Closed Monday and Tuesday.
AIR member

The Flying Frog Café is one of Asheville's most unique upscale dining establishments, featuring a culmination of flavors perfected by more than two decades of Asheville dining history. Owned and operated by veteran restaurateurs Jay and Vijay Shastri, The Flying Frog Café is an eclectic journey through the eyes of a family rich with culture and diversity.

Passionate about great food and wines, Chef/Certified Sommelier Vijay Shastri showcases classical as well as innovative European and Indian cuisines and an impressive list of reviews from almost every major newspaper and culinary magazine in the United States. You also can enjoy their boutique wine list with several hundred vintages of great wines.

pancetta-wrapped squab with pomegranate and madeira

Mix the pomegranate seeds, pomegranate juice, orange juice, wine, orange zest, lemon zest, mint, parsley and basil in a bowl. Add the squabs and marinate in the refrigerator for several hours. Drain the squabs, reserving the liquid and pomegranate seeds. Set the pomegranate seeds aside. Stuff the squabs with most of the pomegranate seeds, reserving some for garnish. Season with salt and pepper. Wrap each in four slices of pancetta.

Preheat the oven to 400 degrees. Cook the squabs in the hot oil in a frying pan until brown. Place in a single layer in a 1-inch-deep baking pan, reserving the oil in the frying pan. Stir the stock and reserved marinade in the reserved oil. Cook over high heat until the mixture is reduced by forty percent, stirring with a spatula to loosen any browned bits. Pour over the squabs and roast for 15 minutes or until cooked through, basting two or three times with the sauce. (You may need to add additional orange juice and wine if the baking pan is getting too dry.) Place the squabs on a serving platter. Season the sauce with salt and pepper and spoon over the squabs. Garnish with the reserved pomegranate seeds.

Flying Frog

1 1/2 cups pomegranate seeds
1/2 cup pomegranate juice
1/2 cup fresh orange juice
1/2 cup good-quality Madeira
2 tablespoons orange zest
1 tablespoon lemon zest
4 to 5 tablespoons chopped
    fresh mint
2 tablespoons Italian
    flat-leaf parsley
1 stem fresh sweet basil
4 (1-pound) whole squabs
Salt and freshly ground pepper
    to taste
16 slices pancetta or bacon
1/2 cup extra-virgin olive oil
1 1/2 cups chicken stock

Serves 4

chef's table

Flying Frog

94

vijay's gingery shrimp and watercress

To prepare the shrimp, preheat the oven to 350 degrees. Place the cumin seeds and coriander seeds separately on a baking sheet and bake until toasted, watching carefully to prevent burning. Grind the seeds in a spice grinder until very fine. Process with the ginger, lemon juice, chiles, cilantro and fenugreek seeds in a blender or food processor until a thick paste forms. Add the oil gradually, processing constantly. Add the yogurt and process until smooth. Stir in salt and add tamarind if you prefer a tart marinade. Pour over the shrimp in a glass bowl. Marinate in the refrigerator for 6 hours or longer. Preheat the grill or preheat the oven to 350 degrees. Place the shrimp on a grill rack or in a baking pan and grill or bake until the shrimp turn pink.

To prepare the salad, blend 1/2 cup olive oil and the lemon juice in a large mixing bowl. Add the onion and watercress and toss to coat. Season with salt. Fry the chiles in oil in a small skillet until the skins begin to blister. Drain on paper towels and season with salt. Arrange the salad on salad plates and top with the shrimp. Garnish with the fried chiles.

shrimp

1/4 cup cumin seeds
1/4 cup coriander seeds
5 (1-inch) pieces fresh ginger
1/3 cup fresh lemon juice
6 hot Thai green chiles
1/3 cup chopped cilantro
2 tablespoons fenugreek
  seeds, ground
1/4 cup vegetable oil
2 cups yogurt
Salt to taste
Tamarind (optional)
2 pounds jumbo shrimp

salad

1/2 cup extra-virgin olive oil
1/4 cup fresh lemon juice
1 white onion, very thinly sliced
1 pound watercress, rinsed
  and trimmed
Salt to taste
Hot green chiles to taste
Vegetable oil or peanut oil
  for frying

Serves 6

chef's table

mountain flavors

Frankie Bones

Chef

Pat Kelly

2 Gerber Road
Asheville, North Carolina 28803
828-274-7111
Web: www.frankiebonesasheville.com
Hours: Lunch 11:30 a.m. – 4:00 p.m.
Monday – Saturday;
Dinner 4:00 p.m. – 10:00 p.m.
Monday – Thursday;
Dinner 4:00 p.m. – 11:00 p.m.
Friday – Saturday;
Dinner 3:00 p.m. – 10:00 p.m. Sunday;
Brunch 10:00 a.m. – 3:00 p.m. Sunday
AIR member

Walk through the door of The Fabulous Frankie Bones and experience the carefree style of early 1960s dining in big cities across America.

At Frankie Bones, snappy sounds, high-back burgundy leather booths, an award-winning menu, and first-class service are the recipe for an experience to remember.

Featuring American-Italian cuisine, Frankie's specializes in hand-cut steaks and chops, fresh seafood, pasta, crisp wheat flatbreads, salads, and appetizers. An extensive wine list is available, and martinis are shaken tableside.

Frankie Bones boasts a casual, smoke-free dining atmosphere with big-city flair. Private dining is available along with takeout and a kid's menu.

Lunch and dinner are served continuously, seven days a week, as well as Sunday brunch. Reservations accepted for dinner.

lobster mac and cheese

Cook the lobster in boiling salted water in a large saucepan for 7 minutes. Remove the lobster immediately to ice water to shock and cool. Remove the meat from the tail and the claws and roughly chop. Reserve the head and tail for garnish. Cook the pasta in boiling salted water in a large saucepan for 12 minutes or until al dente.

Preheat the oven to 350 degrees. Melt the butter in a heavy nonstick skillet. Add the cream and half-and-half. Bring to a simmer and cook for 2 minutes. Add the lobster meat, cooked pasta, Parmesan cheese, Swiss cheese, provolone cheese and fontina cheese. Simmer over medium heat for 3 minutes or until the cheese is combined throughout, stirring constantly. Fold in 1 teaspoon thyme and pepper. Spoon into a 10-inch ovenproof round pasta bowl and dust the top with the bread crumbs. Bake for 5 minutes. Garnish with the reserved lobster head, tail and sprigs of fresh thyme. Serve with Bollini Pino Grigio Reserve.

Note: Use Italian fontina as many other fontina cheeses tend to be younger, softer and blander.

Frankie Bones

1 1/2 pounds live lobster
Salt to taste
4 ounces dry rigatoni
1/4 cup (1/2 stick) butter
1/4 cup heavy cream
1/2 cup half-and-half
1/4 cup (1 ounce) finely grated
    Parmesan cheese
1/4 cup (1 ounce) shredded
    Swiss cheese
1/4 cup (1 ounce) shredded
    provolone cheese
1/4 cup (1 ounce) shredded Italian
    fontina cheese
1 teaspoon fresh thyme leaves
Pepper to taste
1/4 cup fine bread crumbs
Sprigs of fresh thyme for garnish

Serves 2

mountain flavors

Frankie Bones

frankie bones mussels

Scrub the mussels and remove the beards. Sauté the onion, garlic and tomatoes in the butter in a large sauté pan until the onion is translucent. Add the mussels, salt, black pepper, red pepper, oregano and wine. Sauté until the mussels begin to open, discarding any mussels that do not open. Sprinkle with the basil.

18 to 22 Prince Edward Island mussels
2 tablespoons chopped onion
1 tablespoon minced garlic
1 cup chopped tomatoes
1/4 cup (1/2 stick) butter
1 teaspoon salt
1 teaspoon black pepper
1/2 teaspoon crushed red pepper
1 tablespoon dry oregano
1/4 cup white wine
1/4 cup chopped fresh basil

Serves 3

Festivals are a big part of the entertainment scene in Asheville and around the mountains. An example of festivals throughout the area are: Bele Chere, Mountain Dance and Folk Festival, Sourwood Festival, Goombay, Lake Eden Arts Festival, and The Brewgrass Festival.
—Tony Kiss, Asheville Citizen-Times

chef's table

The Grovewood Café

exotic mushroom sauté

Sauté the mushrooms in the olive oil and canola oil in a skillet over medium heat for 3 minutes. Add the leeks, garlic, red pepper flakes, anchovy fillets, parsley and 1/4 cup butter. Sauté over low heat for 2 minutes. Remove the mushrooms with a slotted spoon and set aside for garnish. Stir the vermouth into the drippings in the skillet. Cook for 1 minute over low heat, stirring to deglaze the skillet. Add the mushroom stock, lemon juice, salt and pepper. Cook over high heat for 2 minutes or until reduced. Add the pasta, basil and tomato and bring to a simmer. Finish with the cold butter and pecans. Serve in a small bowl and garnish with the mushrooms.

8 cups mushrooms (morels, chicken of the woods or any combination of wild edible mushrooms, or mushrooms such as cremini, shiitake, or button)

2 tablespoons olive oil

2 tablespoons canola oil

3 tablespoons chopped leeks

1 tablespoon chopped garlic

1/2 teaspoon red pepper flakes

2 teaspoons chopped anchovy fillets

2 tablespoons chopped parsley

1/4 cup (1/2 stick) butter

1/4 cup dry vermouth

4 cups mushroom stock

1/2 teaspoon fresh lemon juice

Salt and pepper to taste

1 cup cooked pasta

2 tablespoons chopped basil

1/2 cup large diced tomato (preferably roasted)

1/4 cup (1/2 stick) butter

2 tablespoons roasted pecans

Serves 2 as an entrée or 4 as an appetizer

chef's table
mountain flavors

Hannah Flanagan's Irish Pub

Owner
Rob Conroy

General Manager
Mark Sternal

27 Biltmore Avenue
Asheville, North Carolina 28801
828-252-1922
www.hannahflanaganspub.net
Hours: Monday – Saturday
11:00 a.m. – 2:00 a.m.;
Sunday Noon – 2:00 a.m.
AIR member

If you are looking for a feisty Irish atmosphere and authentic Irish food, look no further. Come to Hannah Flanagan's, an Irish pub and restaurant in beautiful downtown Asheville. Some of the finest Irish draft and bottled beers around are served. Specialties include authentic fish 'n' chips, corned beef and cabbage, shepherd's pie, steaks, and more.

Hannah Flanagan's was named after the owner's great-grandmother, whose picture still hangs above the bar. Experience the authentic 20th-century-themed interior or enjoy the breeze outside on the ivy-draped terrace.

This is more than a place to eat and drink. Come sing and dance to live music on Thursday, Friday, and Saturday nights, and Sunday in the late afternoon.

Come experience Hannah Flanagan's Pub…where everybody is Irish!

crab dip

Preheat the oven to 350 degrees. Remove the shells from the crab meat. Discard the seeds from the chiles and chop. Sauté the chiles and onion in a nonstick skillet until the onion is translucent. Add the cream cheese, mixed cheese, wine, garlic, cayenne pepper, Old Bay seasoning, basil, thyme, salt, black pepper and blackening seasoning and mix well. Stir in the crab meat. Spoon into an 8×8-inch baking dish. Bake for 10 minutes or until the top is brown and heated through. Serve warm.

2 pounds crab meat
1/2 cup jalapeño chiles
1/2 onion, chopped
24 ounces cream cheese, softened
3/4 cup (3 ounces) shredded
   mixed cheese
2 tablespoons white wine
1 1/2 teaspoons granulated garlic
1 1/2 teaspoons cayenne pepper
1 1/2 teaspoons Old Bay seasoning
1/4 teaspoon each basil and thyme
1 1/2 teaspoons salt
1 1/2 teaspoons black pepper
Blackening seasoning to taste

Serves 10

spinach artichoke dip

Combine the cream cheese, sour cream and lemon juice in a bowl and mix until smooth. Add the garlic, salt and pepper and mix well. Drain the artichoke hearts and chop. Stir the artichoke hearts, spinach and mixed cheese into the cream cheese mixture.

24 ounces cream cheese, softened
2 1/2 cups sour cream
1 1/2 teaspoons lemon juice
1 1/2 tablespoons minced garlic
1 1/2 teaspoons salt
1 tablespoon pepper
5 (8-ounce) cans artichoke hearts
5 cups cooked chopped spinach
1/2 cup (2 ounces) shredded
   mixed cheese

Serves 10

Hannah Flanagan's Irish Pub

chef's table

Hannah Flanagan's Irish Pub

shepherd's pie

Sauté the lamb in a large stockpot until cooked through. Add the beef stock, chicken stock, peas, carrots, rosemary, garlic, salt and pepper and mix well. Melt the butter in a saucepan. Add the flour gradually, whisking constantly until the roux is smooth and the consistency of play dough. (The dough should stick in a clump but not to the pan.) Add to the stock mixture and bring to a boil. Reduce the heat and simmer to the desired consistency. Spoon into the bread bowls and serve.

Note: Bread bowls are available at local bakeries or specialty food stores. You may spoon the mixture into ovenproof bowls.

2 pounds (about) deboned
   leg of lamb
1¹/4 quarts beef stock
1 cup chicken stock
¹/2 small package frozen peas,
   thawed
3 carrots, peeled and sliced
1¹/2 teaspoons rosemary
1¹/2 teaspoons granulated garlic
Salt and pepper to taste
1 cup (2 sticks) butter
¹/2 cup all-purpose flour
4 bread bowls, hollowed out
   (See note)

Serves 4

Hannah Flanagan's Irish Pub

chef's table

Horizons

Chef

Deb Ivey

Grove Park Inn Resort and Spa
Macon Avenue
Asheville, North Carolina
828-252-2711
www.groveparkinn.com
Hours: October – December: nightly;
January – June: Tuesday – Saturday;
July – September: Monday – Saturday.
Jackets are required for gentlemen.
Reservations are recommended.
AIR member

Chef de Cuisine Deb Ivey suggests you and your guests make plans for an evening of pure epicurean adventure at the restaurant that Frommer's hails as "the finest in the area." With dazzling innovations on classic cuisine, a world-class wine list, and impeccable service, the hours you spend at the resort's flagship restaurant add up to more than just a dinner out. If you are hungry for a dining experience that lives up to The Grove Park Inn's historic grandeur, nothing satisfies like a visit to Horizons.

For an incredible behind-the-scenes experience, dine at our Chef's Table in the Horizons kitchen at a table set for you and your guests. Throughout the nine-course dinner, you'll be treated to personal attention from our Chef and Sommelier.

mahi-mahi and lobster macaroni and cheese

Melt the butter in a non-reactive saucepan. Stir in the flour and cook for 3 minutes, stirring constantly. Add the wine and milk and stir until smooth. Bring to a simmer. Add the cheese and cook until melted, stirring constantly. Stir in the lobster meat and pasta and set aside. Heat a sauté pan over medium-high heat. Season the fish with salt and pepper. Sear the fish for 5 minutes on each side. Spoon the macaroni and cheese in the center of each serving plate. Place the fish on top and garnish with fresh herbs.

1/4 cup (1/2 stick) butter
1/4 cup sifted all-purpose flour
1/4 cup white wine
1 cup milk
*1/2 cup (2 ounces) shredded white
    Cheddar cheese*
4 ounces lobster meat, cooked
2 cups penne rigata, cooked
5 (5-ounce) mahi-mahi
Salt and pepper to taste
Fresh herbs for garnish

Serves 5

pineapple flambé with cinnamon ice cream

Temper the ice cream in a large bowl. Stir in the cinnamon. Return to the container or carton and refreeze. Peel and core the pineapple. Cut the pineapple into 1-inch cubes. Heat a sauté pan. Add the butter and brown sugar and heat until smooth, stirring constantly. Add the pineapple and heat until hot, tossing constantly. Remove from the heat and add the rum. Ignite and let the flames subside. Scoop the ice cream into serving bowls and spoon the pineapple mixture over the top.

1/2 gallon vanilla ice cream
2 teaspoons cinnamon
1 fresh pineapple
1/4 cup (1/2 stick) butter
4 ounces brown sugar
*6 ounces Captain Morgan's
    Spiced Rum*

Serves 4 to 6

chef's table
mountain flavors

chef's table

Horizons

110

sautéed shrimp with sweet potato risotto

Preheat the oven to 400 degrees. Roast the sweet potatoes for 50 minutes. Peel the sweet potatoes and mash in a bowl until smooth; set aside. Melt 1/4 cup butter in a non-reactive heavy stockpot. Add the onion and sauté for 5 minutes or until translucent. Add the rice and sauté over low heat for 8 minutes or until the rice turns opaque. Add enough hot broth to cover the rice by one inch, stirring constantly. Cook over medium heat until the broth is absorbed, stirring constantly. Repeat with the remaining broth until almost all of the broth is absorbed and the rice is al dente. Stir in 1/4 cup butter, the sweet potatoes and cheese. Cook until the cheese melts, stirring constantly. Season with salt and pepper. Cover and keep hot over a double boiler.

Heat the olive oil in a medium sauté pan over high heat until the olive oil smokes. Add the shrimp and sauté for 2 minutes. Add the garlic and sauté for 1 minute. Add the wine, stirring to deglaze the pan. Add 1/4 cup butter to bind the sauce and sprinkle with the chives. Spoon the risotto onto serving plates and surround with the shrimp and pan sauce.

2 sweet potatoes, scrubbed
1/4 cup (1/2 stick) butter
1 onion, finely chopped
2 cups arborio rice
10 cups boiling chicken broth
1/4 cup (1/2 stick) butter
3/4 cup (3 ounces) grated fresh
   Parmigiano Romano
Salt and pepper to taste
2 tablespoons olive oil
24 (16- to 20-count) shrimp,
   peeled and deveined
1 tablespoon chopped garlic
1/2 cup white wine
1/4 cup (1/2 stick) butter
2 tablespoons chopped
   fresh chives

Serves 4 to 6

chef's table

mountain flavors

Inn on Church Street

Chef

Michael Atkinson

201 3rd Avenue, West
Hendersonville, North Carolina 28739
828-693-3258
www.innonchurch.com
Hours: Lunch 11:00 a.m. – 2:00 p.m.;
Dinner 5:00 p.m. – 9:00 p.m.;
Brunch 11:00 a.m. – 2:00 p.m.

Hendersonville's Inn on Church Street takes great pride in its historic background as a 1920s inn and its award-winning restaurant. Just one block off Main Street, the Inn is owned by Steve and Brenda Merrefield and managed by Michelle Briggs. The restaurant serves a full breakfast for Inn guests, upscale lunch with outdoor porch dining, an inspired dinner, and Sunday brunch.

Chef Michael Atkinson and his staff strive to showcase seasonally the area's diverse local products such as organic produce, mountain trout, and sourwood honey. The restaurant is dedicated to providing its guests with varied and exciting menus, professional service, wonderfully prepared food, and an extensive wine list. Wines and special theme dinners are a trademark of the restaurant, which has won the Wine Spectator Award for the last several years.

tequila lime sauce

Mix the arrowroot with enough water to form a paste. Melt 1 tablespoon of the butter in a hot saucepan. Add the shallots and cook until tender. Add the tequila and lime juice, stirring to deglaze the saucepan. Add the fish bouillon and the cream. Simmer until the mixture is reduced, thickening with the arrowroot mixture. Stir in cilantro and salt. Whisk in the remaining butter to enrich.

2 tablespoons arrowroot
    or cornstarch
1/2 cup (1 stick) unsalted butter
1 tablespoon finely
    chopped shallots
4 ounces tequila
1/4 cup lime juice
1 cube fish bouillon
1 pint heavy cream
Cilantro to taste
Salt to taste

Makes 1 pint

pico de gallo

Combine the tomatoes, bell peppers, onion, cilantro, lemon juice and kosher salt in a bowl and mix well.

2 ripe tomatoes, seeded
    and chopped
1/2 each green, red and yellow
    bell pepper, finely chopped
1/2 yellow onion, finely chopped
1/2 bunch cilantro, finely chopped
Juice of 1 lemon
Kosher salt to taste

Makes 1 cup

chef's table

Inn on Church Street

114

blackened salmon margarita

Preheat the oven to 350 degrees. Coat the salmon with the blackening seasoning. Melt the unsalted butter in an ovenproof skillet. Add the salmon and cook until blackened on both sides. Splash with white wine and lemon juice and bake until the salmon flakes easily.

Sauté the crab meat in the Dill Butter in a skillet and set aside. Wet your finger with cold water and rub around the rim of a dinner plate. Sprinkle with the sea salt. Ladle the Tequila Lime Sauce in the center of the plate. Arrange the salmon pieces over the sauce and top with the crab meat. Top with Pico de Gallo. Garnish with the chopped cilantro and a wedge of lime.

2 (2- to 3-ounce) pieces salmon,
   tuna or swordfish, cut on
   the bias
1 tablespoon blackening seasoning
1 tablespoon unsalted butter
Splash of white wine
Splash lemon juice
2 ounces lump crab meat
1 tablespoon Dill Butter (below)
1 tablespoon sea salt or kosher salt
4 ounces Tequila Lime Sauce
   (page 113)
2 ounces Pico de Gallo (page 113)
1 teaspoon chopped cilantro
   for garnish
1 lime wedge for garnish

Serves 1

dill butter

Process the butter, dill weed, capers, lemon juice, wine and onion in a food processor until well mixed. Roll in baking parchment to form a log. Chill until firm and cut into slices.

$1/2$ cup (1 stick) unsalted butter,
   softened
1 bunch fresh dill weed
1 tablespoon capers
1 teaspoon lemon juice
1 tablespoon white wine
1 teaspoon chopped red onion

Makes $1/2$ cup

chef's table

mountain flavors

Jack of the Wood

Chef

David Wilson

95 Patton Avenue
Asheville, North Carolina 28801
828-252-3445
www.jackofthewood.com
Hours: Monday – Friday
4:00 p.m. – 2:00 a.m.;
Saturday 12:00 p.m. – 2:00 a.m.;
Sunday 3:00 p.m. – 2:00 a.m.
AIR member

Jack of the Wood is one of Asheville's favorite downtown meeting spots. It's a cozy Celtic pub with a smoke-free, family-friendly atmosphere, featuring high-energy music on weekend nights and unplugged sessions throughout the week.

The food is wholesome, fresh, and traditional, featuring locally grown, hormone-free meats. The handcrafted, English-style, Green Man Ales are brewed at a nearby brewery, and the selection changes according to the season.

irish beef and curry pie

To prepare the pie, preheat the oven to 350 degrees. Sauté the onion in the oil in a medium skillet over medium heat until translucent. Add the garlic and potatoes and cook for 5 minutes. Add the ground beef, cumin, curry powder, pepper, salt and sugar and sauté for 3 minutes. Stir in the soy sauce, water and peas. Reduce the heat and simmer until most of the liquid has evaporated; let cool.

Lay the pastry on a floured surface. Cut into 5-inch circles. (Six circles can be cut from each sheet.) Lightly pack 1/3 cup of the filling onto one-half of the pastry circles, leaving 1/2-inch space around the edges. Gently stretch the remaining pastry circles over the top, moistening the edges and lightly crimping with a fork to seal. Cut 1/2-inch slits in the top of each and brush with the beaten egg. Place on a greased baking sheet and bake for 20 minutes or until golden brown.

To prepare the gravy, bring the Guinness stout, beef base, thyme and onion powder to a boil in a saucepan. Reduce the heat to low and simmer for 20 minutes. Melt the butter in a saucepan and whisk in the flour. Add to the Guinness mixture gently and cook until thickened, stirring constantly. Serve with the pies along with mashed potatoes and vegetables.

pie

3/4 cup chopped yellow onion
3/4 tablespoon soybean oil
1 tablespoon minced garlic
1 potato, cut into 1/4-inch cubes
3/8 pound ground beef
1 tablespoon cumin
1 tablespoon curry powder
1/4 teaspoon pepper
3/4 teaspoon salt
1 teaspoon sugar
3/4 tablespoon soy sauce
3/8 cup water
3/8 cup fresh peas
2 sheets puff pastry
1 egg, beaten

guinness gravy

1/2 pint Guinness stout
1/2 pint beef base
1 teaspoon thyme
1 teaspoon onion powder, or
    1 tablespoon minced onion
2 tablespoons butter
1/4 cup all-purpose flour

Makes 6 pies

chef's table

Jack of the Wood

118

chicken masama curry

Bring the coconut milk, chile, cilantro, red pepper flakes, cumin, coriander, curry powder, basil and salt to a light boil in a saucepan over medium to medium-high heat. Add the potatoes and reduce the heat. Simmer for 15 minutes. Add the chicken, bell pepper, onion and celery. Simmer for 20 minutes or until the chicken is cooked through and the mixture is reduced. Serve over the rice. Garnish with a slice of lime and the dates.

2 (13-ounce) cans unsweetened
   coconut milk
1/4 jalapeño chile, minced
1/2 cup cilantro, finely chopped
1 teaspoon red pepper flakes
1 tablespoon cumin
1 teaspoon coriander
1/4 cup curry powder
2 teaspoons basil
Pinch of salt
1 1/2 baking potatoes, cut into
   1/4-inch pieces
1 chicken breast, chopped
1 bell pepper, cut into pieces
1/4 red onion, finely chopped
3 ribs celery, chopped
1 1/2 cups jasmine rice, cooked
Slice of lime for garnish
3 Medjool dates, julienned into
   small strips for garnish

Serves 4

Jack of the Wood

chef's table
mountain flavors

Kamm's Frozen Custard Shop

Owners

Jim and Sally Kammann

1 Page Avenue
Suite 111
The Grove Arcade
Asheville, North Carolina 28801
828-225-7200
www.bodybalance.com
Hours: Monday – Thursday
12:00 p.m. – 7:00 p.m.;
Friday and Saturday
12:00 p.m. – 9:30 p.m.;
Sunday 1:00 p.m. – 6:00 p.m.
Call for winter hours.
AIR member

What is frozen custard? Technically, it is a type of premium ice cream made with pasteurized egg yolks. For Kamm's customers, it is a delicious, satiny, fresh ice cream delight.

Kamm's Frozen Custard Shop, founded in 2002, was the first business to open in the remodeled Grove Arcade in the historic district of downtown Asheville.

Kamm's Frozen Custard is made fresh throughout the day, offering thousands of combinations of flavors and mix-ins. Kamm's signature treat is the Smash, which combines fresh custard and flavors and/or mix-ins.

Kamm's: "An incredible ice cream experience."

southern comfort pie

Place the frozen custard in a large mixing bowl and let stand until softened. Fold in the pecans, candy and butterscotch topping using a large spoon. Do not overmix. Spoon into the pie shell and smooth the top. Freeze for 2 hours or until set.

To serve, remove from the freezer and let stand at room temperature for 10 to 15 minutes. Cut into wedges.

1 quart frozen vanilla custard

1/3 cup roasted chopped pecans

1/3 cup crushed Heath candy bars

3 tablespoons butterscotch
   topping

1 (9-inch) Oreo or graham
   cracker pie shell

Serves 6 to 8

Kamm's Frozen Custard Shop

Colleges and universities are located throughout Western North Carolina, adding to the region's diversity and cultural attractions. Campuses include Appalachian State University, Asheville-Buncombe Technical Community College, University of North Carolina Asheville, Blue Ridge Community College, Brevard College, Mars Hill College, Montreat College, Warren Wilson College, and Western Carolina University.

—Michael Flynn, Asheville Citizen-Times

chef's table

Kamm's Frozen Custard Shop

122

blueberry and strawberry parfait

Place a layer of frozen custard, a layer of blueberries, a layer of pecans, another layer of frozen custard, a layer of strawberries and another layer of pecans in each of four parfaits or other clear dessert glasses. Repeat the layers in this order until you reach the top of each glass. Garnish with remaining chopped pecans. Freeze until serving time. Let stand for 5 to 10 minutes at room temperature before serving.

Kamm's Frozen Custard Shop

1 pint frozen vanilla custard
1 cup fresh or frozen blueberries
1/4 cup chopped pecans
1 cup fresh or frozen strawberries

Serves 4

chef's table

mountain flavors

La Caterina Trattoria

Owner/Chef

Victor Giancola

39 Elm Street
Asheville, North Carolina 28801
828-254-1148
info@lacaterina.com
Hours: Open for dinner
7 days a week at 5:00 p.m.
AIR member

La Caterina Trattoria was opened in 1994 by Victor Giancola and his wife, Robbin, with the intention of offering the food of Southern Italy with honesty and simplicity. It has grown into a favorite of locals and visitors attracted to the inspired interpretation of this cuisine. Ten extremely successful years later, the restaurant moved from a small storefront to a larger location on 39 Elm Street, providing the chef with a kitchen to complement his skill.

The food at La Caterina is prepared the old-fashioned way, using the best resources, with a commitment to sustainability whenever possible. Rigorously opposed to processed, synthetic, and mass-produced food, the kitchen at La Caterina is dedicated to safeguarding the cuisine of Victor's Italian heritage. Pasta, fresh mozzarella, and cured meats are all produced in-house.

La Caterina preserves the tradition where Italian culture is most vividly celebrated—at the table.

insalata mele e zucca

Remove the cores from two of the apples and reserve. Place the cored unpeeled apples in a bowl filled with a mixture of lemon juice and cool water to cover.

Remove and discard the core from the remaining apple. Chop the apple and place in a stainless steel saucepan. Add the reserved apple cores, cinnamon stick, sugar, peppercorns and enough water to cover. Simmer until the liquid becomes a light syrup. Strain into a stainless steel bowl, discarding the solids. Add the vinegar and blend well. Whisk in 3/4 cup olive oil gradually. Season with the salt and pepper to taste.

Cut the squash into halves and discard the seeds. Peel the squash and julienne. Drain the apples and julienne. Chop the mint. Combine the squash, apples and mint in a bowl and toss to mix. Drizzle lightly with olive oil. Arrange the squash mixture on individual salad plates. Spoon the apple vinaigrette over the top. Garnish with the hazelnuts and cheese.

La Caterina Trattoria

3 Granny Smith apples
Lemon juice
1 cinnamon stick
1 tablespoon sugar
5 peppercorns
2 tablespoons white wine vinegar
3/4 cup olive oil
Pinch of salt, or to taste
Pepper to taste
2 small to medium
    butternut squash
3 sprigs of mint
Olive oil for drizzling (optional)
1/2 cup toasted hazelnuts
    for garnish
Shaved Romano cheese
    for garnish

Serves 8 as an appetizer

chef's table

La Caterina Trattoria

126

gamberi con peperoni misto

Heat a large cast-iron skillet and add the olive oil. Add the garlic and sauté until the garlic begins to brown. Add the bell pepper and cherry peppers and sauté for 2 minutes. Add the cherry tomatoes and sauté until the cherry tomatoes begin to "melt." Add the shrimp and sauté until the shrimp just begin to turn pink. Add the lemon juice, mint and peas and remove from the heat. Drain the hot cooked pasta, reserving a few ounces of the pasta water. Add the pasta and reserved pasta water to the shrimp mixture and toss to mix. Garnish with the parsley and serve in the skillet.

Note: Pickled cherry peppers are found in the pickle section of specialty markets. They have a lot of "heat."

3 to 4 tablespoons olive oil

4 garlic cloves, thinly sliced
    into wafers

3/4 cup chopped red bell pepper

4 or 5 pickled cherry peppers
    (see note)

2 cups cherry tomatoes,
    cut into halves

1 1/2 pounds medium shrimp
    or scallops

Juice of 1/2 lemon

12 fresh mint leaves,
    coarsely chopped

3/4 cup fresh or frozen green peas

16 ounces cappellini,
    cooked al dente

1/4 cup Italian flat leaf parsley,
    coarsely chopped for garnish

Serves 4

chef's table

Laughing Seed

The Laughing Seed Café is a completely vegetarian restaurant specializing in food from around the world with a special unique touch. Locally grown and predominately organic ingredients enliven the cuisine, and recipes are always bursting with bright, exotic flavors. Laughing Seed has been in downtown Asheville for sixteen years and is always coming up with creative ways to make vegan and vegetarian dishes appealing to all.

Chef
Jason Sellers

40 Wall Street
Asheville, North Carolina 28801
828-252-3445
www.laughingseed.com
Hours: Monday, Wednesday, Thursday
11:30 a.m.– 9:00 p.m.; Friday and
Saturday 11:30 a.m. – 10:00 p.m.;
Sunday 10:00 a.m. – 9:00 p.m.
(Brunch 10:00 a.m. – 2:00 p.m.);
Closed on Tuesdays.
AIR member

wild summer fruit gazpacho

Combine the mangoes, papayas, melons, shallots, garlic, chiles, lime juice, vinegar, agave nectar, basil, cilantro, salt, black pepper and cayenne pepper in a mixing bowl and mix well. Pour one-half of the mixture in a blender and purée until almost smooth. Return to the mixing bowl and stir to mix. Adjust the seasonings to taste. Chill for 1 hour before serving.

Ladle the gazpacho into chilled small soup bowls and garnish with avocado slices.

Laughing Seed

4 mangoes, finely chopped
  (preferably Ataulfos
  from Mexico)
2 ripe papayas, finely chopped
2 Magritte melons,
  finely chopped
4 large shallots, minced
4 garlic cloves, minced
4 habanero chiles, minced
Juice of 3 limes
2 tablespoons raw apple
  cider vinegar
3 tablespoons raw agave nectar
1/2 cup packed chopped local
  fresh basil
1/2 cup packed chopped local
  fresh cilantro
Salt and black pepper to taste
Pinch of cayenne pepper, or
  to taste
Thinly sliced avocado for garnish

Serves 8

chef's table

Laughing Seed

130

indian spiced heirloom tomatoes with cultured tofu paneer

Cover the tofu completely with about 1/4 inch of miso. Place on a plate and cover with plastic wrap. Let stand at room temperature or in a warm place for three days or until the tofu smells sweet and sour. Wipe off the miso and cut the tofu into 1/2-inch cubes.

Preheat the oven to 350 degrees. Cut the tops off the tomatoes and scoop out the seeds. Rub the tomatoes with a small amount of oil and place on a baking sheet. Heat 1/4 cup oil in a heavy saucepan over medium heat until the oil shimmers. Add the onion and sweat for 5 minutes. Add the garlic and cumin and cook for 3 minutes. Reduce the heat and add the spinach. Cook for 5 minutes or until the spinach wilts. Stir in the lemon juice, garam masala, salt and white pepper. Remove from the heat and stir in the tofu. Heat 3 tablespoons oil in a sauté pan until the oil shimmers. Add the fennel seeds and sauté over medium-low heat for 8 minutes or until the seeds are soft but not brown. Stir into the spinach mixture.

Stuff each tomato with the mixture and top with the almonds. Bake for 15 to 20 minutes or until the almonds are light brown and the tomatoes soften. Serve over hot rice. Garnish with cilantro.

Laughing Seed

1 (14- to 16-ounce) block
   firm tofu
Sweet white miso for covering
4 large local heirloom tomatoes,
   such as Brandywine or
   German Queen
1/4 cup vegetable oil
1 large yellow onion, sliced
3 tablespoons minced garlic
2 tablespoons freshly
   ground cumin
2 pounds local fresh spinach,
   rinsed and chopped
Juice of 1 lemon
1 tablespoon garam masala mix
Salt and white pepper to taste
3 tablespoons vegetable oil
2 tablespoons large fennel seeds
1 cup whole almonds,
   coarsely ground
Hot cooked basmati rice with
   saffron and pistachios or your
   favorite rice
Chopped fresh cilantro
   for garnish

Serves 4

chef's table

mountain flavors

Laurey's

Owner/Chef

Laurey Masterton

67 Biltmore Avenue
Asheville, North Carolina 28801
828-252-1500; 1-800-YUM-EATS
www.laureysyum.com
Hours: Monday – Friday:
8:00 a.m. – 6:00 p.m.;
Saturday: 8:00 a.m. – 4:00 p.m.
AIR member

Chef and Owner Laurey Masterton grew up in Vermont at Blueberry Hill Inn, learning about fresh, homemade foods from her mother, Elsie Masterton, author of *The Blueberry Hill Cookbooks*.

After a stint in New York City working as a theatrical lighting designer, Laurey moved to Asheville in 1987 where she became an Outward Bound Instructor and, soon after, founded Laurey's.

Laurey's now includes a fifty-plus-seat café in downtown Asheville and a private dining area for special events in addition to the full-service catering company. Home of low-key breakfasts and "Gourmet Comfort Foods," Laurey's is pleased to be a deliciously involved member of this community, supporting local farmers and being fully engaged in making—and serving—a difference.

Don't Postpone Joy®!

john's dunk sauce

Combine the vinegar, lemon juice, horseradish, ketchup, Worcestershire sauce, onion, mayonnaise and salt in a small bowl and mix well. Serve with shrimp, use as a dip with fresh vegetables, as a spread on a sandwich or slathered on an omelet. Store any leftovers in the refrigerator for a week or so.

1 tablespoon vinegar
2 tablespoons lemon juice
2 tablespoons grated horseradish
1/2 cup ketchup
1 tablespoon Worcestershire sauce
1 tablespoon grated onion
1 1/4 cups mayonnaise
1/2 teaspoon salt

Makes about 2 1/4 cups

elsie's tomato seven seasonings

Preheat the oven to 350 degrees. Cut the tomatoes into halves through the "equator," assuming that the stem is the "North Pole." Lay cut side up in a baking pan. Sprinkle each tomato half with 1/4 teaspoon sugar, salt and pepper to taste, 1/8 teaspoon garlic, 1/4 teaspoon basil, a slice of onion and 1/2 teaspoon cheese in the order listed. Bake for 10 minutes or until the cheese is brown, finishing under the broiler, if desired.

Note: This is especially wonderful with fresh "right out of the garden" tomatoes.

2 tomatoes
1 teaspoon sugar
Salt and pepper to taste
1/2 teaspoon granulated garlic
1 teaspoon dried basil
4 thin slices onion
2 teaspoons grated
   Parmesan cheese

Serves 4

chef's table

Laurey's

134

elsie's shrimp tempura

Heat the peanut oil in an electric fry cooker for 3 to 5 minutes or until hot enough to deep-fry. (The way to know if the oil is hot enough is to drop a "strike anywhere" match in the oil when you turn the heat on. These also are known as kitchen matches, but make sure you use the kind with the little white tip—the regular ones will not ignite on their own. When the oil is hot enough, the match will ignite.)

Mix the flour, salt and baking powder in a medium mixing bowl. Add the milk and eggs and mix with a fork just until the batter is barely mixed. (Do not overmix. Do not try to get rid of every tiny lump.) Dip the shrimp into the batter one at a time by holding the tail and lower into the hot oil. (The shrimp will immediately start bubbling and frying.) Deep-fry for 1 minute or until the shrimp floats to the surface. Turn over the shrimp and deep-fry the other side for 1 minute or until light golden brown. Remove to paper towels to drain. Serve with John's Dunk Sauce on page 133.

Note: You may deep-fry 4 or 5 shrimp at a time, but place them in the hot oil one after the other so they fry at almost the same time.

Laurey's

1 quart peanut oil
1 cup all-purpose flour
1 teaspoon salt
1 teaspoon baking powder
1 cup milk
2 eggs, lighty beaten
2 pounds cleaned shrimp with
    tails, peeled and deveined

Serves 15 as an appetizer

chef's table

mountain flavors

Little Venice

Owners/Chefs

Steve and Kim Servais

800 Fairview Road
Suite 9
Asheville, North Carolina 28803
828-299-8911
Hours: Monday – Thursday
11 a.m. – 9 p.m.
Friday – Saturday
11:00 a.m. – 10:00 p.m.
Sunday, 12:00 p.m. – 3:30 p.m.
AIR member

A fun and friendly atmosphere awaits you at Little Venice Pizzeria and Bar, an Asheville favorite for more than ten years.

Aside from the wonderful New York style pizza, Little Venice offers an array of appetizers, soups and salads, pasta, sub favorites, and selections from the Greek corner. It is famous for homemade sauces, pastas, Greek salad, and pizzas. Fresh, local ingredients are served up in a cozy atmosphere great for couples and families. Come and see the newly remodeled dining room. Visit the Gondola Lounge with nightly specials and full ABC permits. A private dining room is available for groups, parties, celebrations, and meetings. A wide range of catering options is available. Join the VIP Club and receive special offers throughout the year. Kid's menus are available.

gondolini

Mix the gin and cocktail infusion mix with ice in a shaker. Swirl the vermouth in a chilled martini glass and discard. Place the cherry in the bottom of the glass and strain the martini into the glass. Serve and enjoy.

1^{1}/2 shots gin or vodka

Splash of Roses Blue Raspberry
cocktail infusion mix

Drop of dry vermouth, or to taste

Whole red maraschino cherry

Serves 1

greek quesadilla

Preheat the grill. Place the chicken on a grill rack and grill until cooked through. (If you prefer the steak or vegetable assortment, grill to the desired degree of doneness.) Chop the chicken into pieces. Layer the mozzarella cheese, feta cheese and tomato on the tortilla and place on the grill rack. Grill until the cheeses melt. Place the chicken over one-half of the tortilla and fold the other half over the top to form a half moon shape. Grill until heated through, turning once. Remove from the grill and cut into quarters. Serve immediately with desired sauce for dipping.

2 chicken tenders, sliced steak or
vegetable assortment

1/4 cup (1 ounce) shredded
mozzarella cheese

Large pinch of crumbled
feta cheese

1 slice tomato, chopped

1 flour tortilla

Red salsa, salsa verde or tzatziki
sauce for dipping

Serves 1

chef's table

Little Venice

138

baked ziti **with** marinara sauce

Preheat the oven to 350 degrees. Cook the pasta in a saucepan using the package directions until al dente. Drain and pour into a large bowl. Add the garlic, oregano, salt, pepper, marinara sauce, bell pepper, onion, ricotta cheese, Parmesan cheese and one-half of the mozzarella cheese and mix well. Spoon into a greased baking pan and sprinkle with the remaining mozzarella cheese. Cover with foil and bake for 30 minutes or until hot and bubbly. Remove the foil and bake for 15 minutes longer or until the mozzarella cheese melts and is golden brown on top. Let stand before serving.

Notes: If using your own homemade marinara sauce, you may need to omit the spices, bell peppers and onion if they are already in your sauce.

Variations: For Baked Ziti with Ground Beef Sauce, substitute meat sauce for the marinara sauce and add crumbled cooked ground beef.

Little Venice

1 pound ziti or penne

1/2 to 1 teaspoon granulated garlic

1/2 to 1 teaspoon oregano

1/2 to 1 teaspoon salt

1/2 to 1 teaspoon freshly ground pepper

3 to 4 cups marinara sauce

1/2 cup chopped green bell pepper

1/2 cup chopped onion

1 cup ricotta cheese

1/4 cup (1 ounce) grated Parmesan cheese

2 cups (8 ounces) shredded mozzarella cheese

Serves 6

chef's table

The Lobster Trap

Chef

Tres Hundertmark

35 Patton Avenue
Asheville, North Carolina 28801
828-350-0505
www.thelobstertrap.biz
Hours: Open at 5:00 p.m. daily
AIR member

Owner Amy Beard grew up on the docks of Portland, Maine, selling lobsters, camping on islands, and filling her belly with lobster and clams. The beauty and peace of the Blue Ridge Mountains lured her away from her home state but could not diminish her passion for the sweet taste of Maine lobster. During a visit with Captain Tom, a high school friend and lobsterman, Amy asked what he thought about sending his daily catch to Asheville to share with her friends. Captain Tom exclaimed, "I can send lobster right off the boat whenever you want!" She wanted her friends to experience the feel of a Maine lobster shack, while taking advantage of the unique culture in Asheville. Enjoy the little place in Asheville where love for the mountains meets love for the sea.

crab and sweet potato soup

Sauté the onion and garlic in the olive oil in a large stockpot until the onion is translucent. Add the sweet potatoes, water, sherry, lemon juice, orange juice, hoisin sauce, coriander, cloves, nutmeg, cayenne pepper, salt and white pepper and bring to a simmer. Simmer for 1 hour or until the sweet potatoes are tender. Purée the soup with an immersion blender. Stir in the crab meat. Ladle into soup bowls.

1/2 yellow onion, chopped
1 ounce garlic, minced
2 tablespoons olive oil
2 pounds sweet potatoes, chopped
1/2 gallon water
1 1/2 cups sherry
1/4 cup lemon juice
1/4 cup fresh orange juice
1 tablespoon hoisin sauce
1 tablespoon coriander, ground
2 whole cloves
1 teaspoon ground nutmeg
1/2 teaspoon cayenne pepper
1 teaspoon salt
1/2 teaspoon white pepper
1 pound crab claw meat

Serves 6 to 8

hickory plank salmon

Preheat the grill. Cook the syrup, vinegar, green onion, red pepper flakes and garlic in a small saucepan until reduced by one-half. Season the fish with salt and pepper. Place flesh side down on a grill rack with four 4- to 6-inch hickory planks and grill for 3 minutes. Turn both and grill for 3 minutes. Place the fish on the planks and brush with the glaze. Grill, covered, or bake in a preheated 400-degree oven for 6 minutes.

1/4 cup Shagbark Hickory syrup
1/4 cup rice wine vinegar
Tops of 1 green onion, chopped
1/4 teaspoon red pepper flakes
1 teaspoon garlic
4 (8-ounce) salmon fillets
Salt and pepper to taste

Serves 4

chef's table
mountain flavors

chef's table

Lobster Trap

142

lobster newburg

Melt ¹/4 cup butter in a sauté pan. Add the shallots and cook until tender. Add the lobster meat and cook until heated through. Add the sherry and cook until almost evaporated, stirring to deglaze the pan. Add the cream and cook until the liquid is reduced and thick. Season with sea salt and pepper. Remove from the heat and whisk in 2 tablespoons butter. Spoon into the pastry shells and serve.

Photograph at left.

1/4 cup (¹/2 stick) butter
1 ounce shallots
2 steamed Maine lobsters,
    coarsely chopped
6 tablespoons sherry
3/4 cup heavy cream
1 teaspoon sea salt
¹/2 teaspoon freshly ground pepper
2 tablespoons butter, softened
2 puff pastry shells

Serves 2

oyster stew

Cook the bacon in a saucepan until the fat is rendered. Remove the bacon and reserve for another purpose. Sweat the shallots in the bacon drippings. Add the spinach and oysters in liquor and cook until the edges of the oysters curl. Add the cream and half-and-half and bring to a simmer. Season with salt and pepper. Ladle evenly into four soup cups. Top with the butter and oyster crackers.

4 ounces bacon or lardons
2 tablespoons minced shallots
2 ounces fresh spinach leaves
1 pint oysters in liquor
1 pint heavy cream
1 pint half-and-half
Salt and pepper to taste
¹/4 cup (¹/2 stick) butter, softened
12 oyster crackers

Serves 4

chef's table
mountain flavors

Mack Kells

Kitchen Manager

Mike Lappin

160 Tunnel Road
Asheville, North Carolina 28805
(828) 253-8805
Hours: Monday – Saturday
11:30 a.m. – 2:00 a.m.;
Sunday 12:00 p.m. – 2:00 a.m.
AIR member

Mack Kells, in Asheville since 1981, is considered to be the original sports and biker bar in town. It is a good place to hang out with friends or co-workers and watch the game or the race. It has a very simple atmosphere and menu, and they like it like that—keeping life down-to-earth and uncomplicated.

If you want great wings of any spice or sauce, a beer to wash them down, and people to talk to, Mack Kells is the place to be and be seen. Ride your bike over for a visit.

mack kells' buffalo wing sauce

Melt the butter in a large saucepan. Stir in the hot sauce and mix well.

3 cups (6 sticks) salted sweet
  cream butter
2 quarts Texas Pete hot sauce

Makes 11 cups

mack kells' spicy teriyaki wing sauce

Combine the teriyaki glaze, honey, red pepper and cayenne pepper in a saucepan and mix well. Cook over medium heat for 4 minutes, stirring frequently.

2 quarts Kikkoman teriyaki glaze
1 quart honey
1/2 cup crushed red pepper
1/4 teaspoon cayenne pepper

Makes 3 quarts

chef's table

mountain flavors

Mack Kells

mack kells' famous chicken wings

Preheat oil in a deep fryer to 350 degrees. Add the chicken wings and deep-fry until cooked through; drain. Toss the chicken wings with buffalo sauce or teriyaki sauce in a bowl. Serve with salad dressing and celery.

Vegetable oil for frying
4 pounds jumbo chicken wings, rinsed and drained
Mack Kells' Buffalo Wing Sauce or Mack Kells' Spicy Teriyaki Wing Sauce (page 145) for tossing
Blue cheese salad dressing or ranch salad dressing
Celery sticks

Makes 4 pounds

The city of Asheville is at the confluence of the French Broad and Swannanoa rivers. The French Broad, which flows north, is thought to be older than the Appalachian chain. The river has its modern name because it flowed into former French territory.

chef's table

The Market Place

Owner/Chef

Mark Rosenstein

20 Wall Street
Asheville, North Carolina 28801
828-252-4162
www.marketplace-restaurant.com
Hours: Monday – Saturday
5:30 p.m. – until.
Check for seasonal hours.

The Market Place Restaurant, on charming Wall Street in the heart of downtown Asheville, has established itself over the past twenty-eight years as a world-class restaurant, acclaimed by publications ranging from the *New York Times* and *Food & Wine* to *Bon Appetit*, *Southern Living* and *Wine Spectator*.

The Market Place restaurant opened in 1979. Chef/owner Mark Rosenstein has continually worked to create a menu based on local products, working closely with Western North Carolina farmers, gardeners, cheese-makers, and wild foragers. The Market Place has been recognized locally, regionally, and nationally for its creative cuisine and dedication to the revival of "taste" based on local foodstuffs and traditional methods.

The chef believes that breaking bread is a celebratory ritual, cooking and serving food are acts of love, and those who gather to eat and drink at his table deserve a divine experience.

crispy potato pancake with applesauce and goat cheese

Preheat a heavy skillet over medium heat. Toss the potatoes with one-half of the melted butter in a bowl. Add the remaining melted butter to the skillet. Divide the grated potatoes into eighteen equal portions. Drop into the heated butter and fry for 5 minutes on each side or until crispy; drain.

Cook the shallots in the vinegar in a saucepan over medium heat until the vinegar is reduced by two-thirds. Add the cider and cook until reduced by one-half. Add the cream and reduce the heat. Simmer the sauce for 15 minutes.

Preheat the oven to 375 degrees. Make six three-cake-high stacks consisting of a potato cake, portion of the goat cheese, dollop of the applesauce, another potato cake, another portion of goat cheese, another dollop of applesauce, another potato cake and ending with a dollop of applesauce. Place in an ovenproof dish and bake for 8 minutes to reheat.

Just before serving, stir the mustard and 3 tablespoons chives into the sauce. Spoon a small amount of the sauce onto each serving plate. Place a potato cake stack on the sauce and top each with a dollop of applesauce. Garnish with additional chives.

The Market Place

4 large potatoes, peeled and grated
10 tablespoons clarified butter, melted
2 shallots, peeled and finely chopped
2 tablespoons cider vinegar
1/2 cup fresh apple cider
1/2 cup heavy cream
6 ounces Spinning Spider fresh goat cheese, cut into twelve 1/2-ounce portions
1 1/2 cups homemade applesauce
1 tablespoon grainy mustard
3 tablespoons chopped fresh chives plus additional for garnish

Serves 6

chef's table

The Market Place

pan-seared fillet of trout with black walnuts

Make a stock by cooking the fish fumet and cider in a saucepan until the mixture is reduced by twenty percent. Pulse the walnuts, flour, salt and pepper in a food processor to form a coarse meal. Dip the fish in butter, shaking off the excess. Dredge in the walnut flour, pressing to adhere. Sauté in butter in a heavy skillet over medium heat for 3 to 4 minutes on each side or until golden brown. Remove to a warm serving plate. Wipe the excess flour from the skillet. Add the whiskey, stirring to deglaze the skillet. Stir in the stock and herbs. Pour over the fish and serve.

Photograph at left.

1 cup fish fumet
2 tablespoons cider
3/4 cup black walnuts
1/4 cup all-purpose flour
Salt and pepper to taste
4 (5-ounce) trout fillets
Melted clarified butter for
    dredging and sautéing
1 tablespoon Jack Daniels whiskey
2 tablespoons chopped parsley
1 tablespoon fresh marjoram

Serves 4

The Market Place

sour cherry soup

Bring the cherries, cinnamon sticks, sugar and water to a boil in a non-aluminum saucepan over medium heat, stirring occasionally. Boil for 5 minutes. Add the wine and return to a boil. Reduce the heat and simmer for 5 minutes. Discard the cinnamon sticks. Let cool and chill. To serve, stir in the half-and-half. Ladle into serving bowls and garnish with mint.

1 pound fresh sour cherries, pitted
2 cinnamon sticks
1/4 cup sugar
2 tablespoons water
2 cups dry red wine
2 cups half-and-half
Sprigs of fresh mint for garnish

Serves 6

chef's table

mountain flavors

Mela Indian Restaurant

Owner/Chef

Anoop Krishnan

70 North Lexington Avenue
Asheville, North Carolina 28801
828-225-8880
www.melaasheville.com
Hours: Lunch buffet
11:30 a.m. – 2:30 p.m.;
dinner 5:30 p.m. – 9:30 p.m. or later.
Open seven days a week.
AIR member

Asheville's only downtown Indian restaurant, Mela has been voted Western North Carolina's "Best Indian Restaurant" by readers of the *Asheville Citizen-Times* and the *Mountain XPress*. Owner Anoop Krishnan insists on authenticity. Spices—anise, coriander, cinnamon, cloves, cumin, fenugreek, red chiles—are freshly roasted and ground each day. Fresh curry leaves flavor rice and curries. Yogurt is made from scratch on site. Naan breads are hand-kneaded and fired in an authentic clay tandoor oven.

The restaurant's interior displays as much character as the food. Visitors pass through an enormous carved wooden door into a dining room graced by other antiques brought from India— a towering carved bar and paintings of Mughal nobility. The space vibrates with color and scent, and on many evenings, with entertainment as varied as belly dancing and cello music. An extensive wine and beer list and imaginative cocktail specials complete the Mela experience.

kashmir chicken curry

Process the bell peppers, onion, ginger, garlic, almonds, 1 tablespoon cilantro, the lemon juice, water, cayenne pepper and black pepper in a blender until a paste forms. Cut the chicken into 2-inch cubes. Heat the canola oil in a skillet. Add the bell pepper paste and cook until the paste begins to bubble. Add the chicken and cook over low to medium heat for 30 minutes or until cooked through. Garnish with cilantro.

3 red bell peppers, cut up
1 large yellow onion, cut up
3 ounces chopped ginger
4 garlic cloves
3 ounces almonds
1 tablespoon chopped
    fresh cilantro
1/4 cup fresh lemon juice
1/4 cup water
1/2 teaspoon cayenne pepper
1/2 teaspoon freshly ground
    black pepper
1 1/2 pounds chicken breasts
2 tablespoons canola oil
Cilantro for garnish

Serves 4

chef's table

Mela Indian Restaurant

154

sweet baked rice

Roast the saffron threads in a skillet over low heat for 4 to 5 minutes. Grind into a fine powder. Add to the warm milk and let stand for 30 minutes. Rinse and drain the rice three or four times. Soak the rice in water to cover in a bowl for 1 hour; drain. Let the rice "breathe" in air for 1 hour.

Preheat the oven to 300 to 325 degrees. Melt the butter in a skillet. Add the cardamom, sugar and cinnamon. Cook for 2 to 3 minutes, stirring constantly. Add $2^{1}/4$ cups water and the rice. Cook until the water is absorbed, stirring constantly. Remove the cinnamon stick and cardamom pods and discard. Spoon the rice into a baking dish. Pour the saffron milk over the top and bake for 30 minutes.

1 teaspoon saffron threads
$1/4$ cup warm milk
2 cups uncooked basmati rice
1 tablespoon salted butter
6 cardamom pods
10 tablespoons sugar
2 cinnamon sticks
$2^{1}/4$ cups water

Serves 6

Mela Indian Restaurant

chef's table
mountain flavors

Mountain Brew

Owner/Chef

Kelly Sharp

3480 Sweeten Creek Road
Asheville, North Carolina 28704
828-687-9009
Hours: Monday – Friday
7:00 a.m. – 4:00 p.m.;
Saturday 8:00 a.m. – 3:00 p.m.
Serving breakfast, lunch, and
sweet treats.

Kelly and Gena met as nurses in the community of Asheville. They had a dream to offer interesting fun food at a reasonable price.

Adding to her chef background, Kelly honed her culinary skills at AB Tech; Gena possessed café experience. Using their passion, they opened their café on Sweeten Creek Road to serve a much-needed niche in a growing area. They buy their produce locally, serve organic coffees, and offer healthy choices as well as guilty pleasures.

Kelly's baked goods have won awards at the Chocolate Festival, and you can find her treats in other restaurants in Asheville. She has also been on WLOS' *Carolina Kitchen* as a frequent guest chef. Come on down and experience a little bit of south Asheville.

quiche in puff pastry shell

Preheat the oven to 350 degrees. Place jumbo silicone baking cups into jumbo muffin cups. Cut the puff pastry into circles and fit into the baking cups to form a shell. Whip the eggs and whipping cream in a bowl. Place spinach and cheese in each pastry shell. Pour the egg mixture over the top of each. Bake for 15 to 20 minutes or until golden brown.

Note: These can be cooled and heated as needed.

Mountain Brew

1 sheet puff pastry
6 to 8 eggs
2 to 3 tablespoons heavy
   whipping cream
Cooked fresh spinach
Crumbled cheese, such as
   Cheddar cheese, feta cheese,
   smoked provolone cheese, etc.

Makes 6

key lime puffs

Preheat the oven to 350 degrees. Combine the condensed milk, egg yolks and Key lime juice in a bowl and mix well. Cut the puff pastry into squares and top each with 1 to 2 teaspoons of the Key lime mixture. Brush the sides of each square with the beaten egg. Fold over and pinch together to seal. Place on a baking sheet and bake for 8 to 10 minutes or until puffy and golden. Let cool and dust with confectioners' sugar.

1 (14-ounce) can sweetened
   condensed milk
2 egg yolks
1/4 to 1/2 cup Key lime juice
1 sheet puff pastry
Beaten egg for brushing
Confectioners' sugar for dusting

Makes 6

chef's table

Mountain Brew

158

chocolate indulgence

This icing can be used on top of your favorite cake recipe. I use it on top of my award-winning Devil's Food Cake recipe made in my café.

To prepare the ganache, melt the chocolate chips with the cream in a saucepan over medium heat, stirring constantly. Cook until thickened, stirring constantly to prevent burning.

To prepare the icing, beat the cream cheese and whipped topping in a mixing bowl at low speed until smooth and creamy. Add the ganache until the desired chocolate taste is reached. Use to frost your favorite cake.

Note: The remaining ganache can be used to drizzle on top of the frosted cake.

Mountain Brew

ganache
1 cup (6 ounces) semisweet
    chocolate chips
1 cup heavy cream

icing
8 ounces cream cheese, softened
12 ounces whipped topping
2 to 6 tablespoons Ganache

Makes enough icing to frost a three-layer cake

chef's table

mountain flavors

Old Europe Bistro

Chef

Joel Bishop

41 North Lexington Avenue
Asheville, North Carolina 28801
828-252-0001
www.oldeuropeasheville.com
Hours: 9:30 a.m. – 10:00 p.m. daily
AIR member

Welcome to a restful destination from the hustle and bustle of everyday life, a place to relax with family and friends, a place to enjoy a true European experience. Hungarian owners Zoltan and Melinda Vetro have brought the true European bistro experience into the heart of downtown Asheville. Tucked into a carefully renovated space on the ground floor of a turn-of-the-century building, the restaurant provides a warm and inviting atmosphere for the dining pleasure of all our guests. Old Europe, an authentic European bistro, is comfortable and inviting. It's a place where locals gather and travelers seek for its unique atmosphere and outstanding yet comfortingly familiar food. A bistro isn't just a restaurant; it is a culmination of great food, friends, and good times. Sit back, relax, and experience a piece of Old Europe.

cream of vidalia onion soup

Sweat the onions in the clarified butter in a small stockpot over medium-low heat for 10 minutes or until tender. (Do not brown.) Add the wine and sweat for 5 minutes. Add the stock and bring to a boil. Reduce the heat and simmer for 10 minutes. Melt 10 tablespoons butter in a sauté pan. Whisk in the flour to form a roux. Cook for 5 minutes, whisking constantly. Add to the onion mixture and mix well to prevent lumps from forming. Remove from the heat and stir in the half-and-half. Season with salt and white pepper. Stir in the sugar. Ladle into soup bowls. Garnish with fried Vidalia onions and parsley.

7 pounds Vidalia onions or other sweet onions, sliced
1/4 cup clarified butter
2 cups white wine
3 quarts vegetable or chicken stock
10 tablespoons butter
5 ounces all-purpose flour
1 1/2 cups half-and-half
Salt and white pepper to taste
2 tablespoons sugar (optional)
Fried Vidalia onions for garnish
Parsley for garnish

Makes 1 gallon

Old Europe Bistro

crab dip

Remove any shells that might remain in the crab meat. Combine the crab meat, cream cheese, sour cream, garlic powder, onion powder, Old Bay seasoning, cayenne pepper, salt and black pepper in a mixing bowl and mix gently with a spatula. Chill, covered, until ready to serve. Heat the dip gently in a saucepan and spoon into a serving bowl. Serve with flat bread chips and a spicy marinara.

1 1/2 pounds lump crab meat, drained
20 ounces cream cheese, softened
1 1/2 cups sour cream
1 tablespoon garlic powder
1 tablespoon onion powder
1 1/2 tablespoons each Old Bay seasoning and cayenne pepper
Salt and black pepper to taste

Serves 12

chef's table

Old Europe Bistro

162

hazelnut-encrusted trout with pear chutney

To prepare the chutney, combine the pears, onion, pear nectar, raisins, vinegar, cranberries, sugar, mustard seeds, ginger, salt and cinnamon stick in a saucepan. Bring to a boil and reduce the heat. Simmer for 45 minutes. Discard the cinnamon stick. Add a little water to the chutney to adjust the consistency, if needed. Chill in the refrigerator for up to 2 weeks. (This will make 3 cups.)

To prepare the trout, mix the bread crumbs and hazelnuts together on a half sheet pan. Lay the trout skin side down and lightly pat dry with a paper towel. Season with salt and pepper. Dredge both sides of the trout in the flour and shake to remove the excess. Dip the flesh side of the trout in the egg wash and shake to remove the excess. Place flesh side down in the bread crumb mixture and press firmly. Let stand for 10 minutes.

Heat the butter in a sauté pan over medium heat. Place the trout encrusted side down and sauté for 3 to 4 minutes or until golden brown. Turn and sauté for 2 minutes. Place the trout on a serving plate. Drain the oil from the sauté pan. Heat 3/4 cup of the chutney in the sauté pan to 140 degrees on a candy thermometer. Top the trout with the warm chutney.

pear chutney

3 cups Bosc pears or other firm
　pears, peeled and chopped
1 large red onion, chopped
2 cups pear nectar or pear juice
1 cup golden raisins
3/4 cup cider vinegar
1/2 cup dried cranberries
1/3 cup sugar
2 tablespoons mustard seeds
2 tablespoons minced fresh ginger
1/4 teaspoon salt
1 cinnamon stick

trout

1/4 cup panko
　(Japanese bread crumbs)
1/2 cup hazelnuts, finely chopped
　in a food processor
4 pan dressed rainbow trout
Salt and pepper to taste
1/4 cup all-purpose flour
1/2 cup egg wash
1/4 cup clarified butter
3/4 cup Pear Chutney

Serves 4

chef's table

mountain flavors

PICHOLINE CAFÉ AND WINE BAR

Chef

Traci Taylor

64 Haywood Street
Asheville, North Carolina 28801
828-254-3800
Hours: Monday – Saturday
7:00 a.m. – 9:00 p.m.;
Sunday 8:00 a.m. – 9:00 p.m.
AIR member

Just a short walk down Haywood Street from the Thomas Wolfe Auditorium and the Asheville Civic Center, PICHOLINE offers the perfect complement to a concert evening.

Traci and Treavis Taylor of Everyday Gourmet Catering and fig bistro are proud to introduce an exciting new café and wine bar in downtown Asheville: PICHOLINE. Serving Haywood Street morning, noon, and night, PICHOLINE offers breakfast all day; a simple yet sophisticated lunch menu; and tapas, appetizers, and petite entrees in the evening. The defining factor at PICHOLINE is attention to detail. Servers are knowledgeable and professional, the ambiance is comfortable yet elegant, and the offerings are of the finest quality available.

sesame salmon

Combine the tamari, vinegar, lemon juice, sesame oil, oyster sauce, fish sauce, chili paste, scallions and ginger in a bowl and mix well. Pour one-third of the sauce over the salmon in a baking dish and sprinkle with the bread crumbs. Pour the remaining sauce carefully over the bread crumbs to evenly cover. Let stand for 30 minutes.

Preheat the oven to 500 degrees. Roast the salmon for 18 to 20 minutes or until the center registers 120 degrees on a meat thermometer. Remove from the oven and let stand for 15 minutes. Place the salmon on a serving platter. Garnish with chopped chives.

PICHOLINE CAFÉ AND WINE BAR

1 cup tamari
1/4 cup rice vinegar
1/4 cup lemon juice
2 teaspoons dark toasted
   sesame oil
3 tablespoons oyster sauce
1 tablespoon fish sauce
1 1/2 teaspoons chili paste
1/2 cup chopped scallions
2 tablespoons minced fresh ginger
2 1/4 pounds salmon fillets
1 1/2 cups fine bread crumbs
Chopped chives, chervil or
   parsley for garnish

Serves 4 to 6

chef's table

mountain flavors

PICHOLINE CAFÉ AND WINE BAR

traci's gazpacho with herbed croutons

To prepare the gazpacho, combine the cucumbers, bell peppers, tomatoes, onions and scallions in a large bowl. Add the garlic, parsley, vegetable juice cocktail, Bloody Mary mix, beef broth, vinegar, Tabasco sauce, salt and black pepper and mix well. Chill for 8 to 10 hours before serving.

To prepare the croutons, preheat the oven to 350 degrees. Roughly chop the bread. Mix the butter and thyme in a large bowl. Add the bread and toss to coat. Spread on a baking sheet. Bake for 15 minutes or until golden brown. Serve with the gazpacho.

gazpacho

2 seedless cucumbers, coarsely chopped

1 red bell pepper, coarsely chopped

1 yellow bell pepper, coarsely chopped

8 plum tomatoes, coarsely chopped

2 red onions, coarsely chopped

1/4 cup chopped scallions

6 garlic cloves, chopped

2 tablespoons chopped parsley

2 cups vegetable juice cocktail

2 cups Bloody Mary mix

1/2 cup beef broth

1/2 cup red wine vinegar

Dash of Tabasco sauce

Salt and cracked black pepper to taste

herbed croutons

Focaccia bread

1/2 cup (1 stick) butter, melted

1 tablespoon thyme

Serves 6

chef's table

mountain flavors

Pomodoros Greek & Italian Café

Chef
Christopher Hadley

Proprietor
Tommy Tsiros

1070 Tunnel Road
Asheville, North Carolina 28805
www.pomodoroscafe.com
Hours: Sunday 10:00 a.m. – 9:30 p.m.;
Monday – Thursday
11:00 a.m. – 9:30 p.m.;
Friday and Saturday
11:00 a.m. – 10:00 p.m.
AIR member

Pomodoros Greek and Italian Café is a full-service restaurant featuring fresh Greek and Italian cuisine, an extensive wine list, a full bar, catering, and friendly service. Pomodoros offers three separate menus of diverse and innovative dishes drawing inspiration from the Mediterranean region of Greece and Italy. The focus is on using fresh ingredients of high quality, from the fresh seafood brought in daily to the freshly picked rosemary. The basis of each dish is always in the tradition of the region, but the ingredients guide the way to new delights as well as old favorites.

trout with crab rémoulade

To prepare the root vegetables, preheat the oven to 425 degrees. Line a baking sheet with baking parchment. Chop the vegetables into 1/2-inch cubes. Mix the olive oil, rosemary, kosher salt and pepper in a large bowl. Add the vegetables and toss to coat. Spread on the prepared baking sheet and roast for 45 minutes.

To prepare the crab rémoulade, mix the mayonnaise, lemon juice, capers, onion, bell pepper, parsley, crab meat, cayenne pepper, sea salt and black pepper in a bowl. Chill, covered, until ready to serve.

To prepare the trout, preheat a gas grill or charcoal grill. Lightly rub each fillet with olive oil and season with sea salt and pepper. Place flesh side down on a grill rack and grill over high heat for 2 to 3 minutes. Turn the fillet 90 degrees to achieve restaurant-style grill marks and grill for 2 minutes longer. Turn the fish over and grill for 3 to 4 minutes or until the fillets are tender and flaky.

Serve with the vegetables and top with the crab rémoulade. Suggested greens to accompany this entrée are sautéed spinach or kale.

Note: The trout may be pan-seared or broiled in the oven.

roasted root vegetables

3 red beets
1 sweet potato, peeled
2 large carrots, peeled
2 Yukon gold potatoes
2 to 3 tablespoons extra-virgin olive oil
2 tablespoons chopped fresh rosemary
Kosher salt and pepper to taste

crab rémoulade

1 cup low-fat canola oil mayonnaise
1/4 cup fresh lemon juice
1 tablespoon capers
1/4 cup minced red onion
1/4 cup minced red bell pepper
1 tablespoon chopped parsley
4 ounces pasteurized lump crab meat
Pinch of cayenne pepper
Sea salt and black pepper to taste

trout

4 (8- to 10-ounce) Sunburst natural trout fillets, pin bone cut
1 tablespoon extra-virgin olive oil
Sea salt and pepper to taste

Serves 4

Pomodoros Greek & Italian Café

chef's table **169**
mountain flavors

chef's table

Pomodoros Greek & Italian Café

melitzanes papoutsakia

Preheat the oven to 350 degrees. Remove the top from the eggplant and cut into halves lengthwise. Lightly brush the flesh of the eggplant with olive oil and season with salt and pepper. Place skin sides down in a baking dish and cover with foil. Bake for 1 hour or until tender but not mushy.

Heat 2 tablespoons extra-virgin olive oil in a large skillet. Add the garlic and leek and sauté until tender. Add the mushrooms and sauté until almost tender. (The mushrooms should still have some plumpness; do not over cook.) Add the wine, stirring to deglaze the skillet. Remove from the heat. Add the artichoke hearts, olives, sun-dried tomatoes, feta cheese, 1/4 cup Parmigiano-Reggiano and the basil and oregano and mix well.

Increase the baking temperature to 450 degrees. Place about 3/4 cup stuffing on each eggplant, mounding firmly with your hand. Bake for 10 to 15 minutes or until a light crust forms on the stuffing. Remove carefully from the oven and garnish with 2 tablespoons shredded Parmigiano-Reggiano and 1 tablespoon fresh herbs.

2 large eggplant

Extra-virgin olive oil for brushing

Salt and pepper to taste

2 tablespoons extra-virgin
    olive oil

2 garlic cloves, thinly sliced

1 leek, finely chopped

2 portobello mushrooms,
    finely chopped

2 tablespoons dry white wine

1 cup quartered artichoke hearts

1/2 cup pitted kalamata
    olives, chopped

1/2 cup sun-dried tomatoes,
    julienned

1/2 cup crumbled feta cheese

1/4 cup (1 ounce) shredded
    Parmigiano-Reggiano

2 tablespoons chopped fresh basil
    and oregano

2 tablespoons shredded
    Parmigiano-Reggiano

1 tablespoon fresh herbs

Serves 4

chef's table

Province 620

Owner

Christ Barlas

620 Hendersonville Road
Asheville, North Carolina 28803
828-277-0355
www.province620.com
Hours: Sunday – Friday
11:00 a.m. – 10:00 p.m.;
Saturday 4:00 p.m. – 10:00 p.m.

Province 620 is a unique, upscale, casual dining restaurant offering more than one hundred menu selections including appetizers, pasta, seafood, steaks, salads, sandwiches, and more. Some of the specialty dishes: Cranberry Mandarin Orange Chicken, Ginger Sesame Seed Encrusted Salmon, Mediterranean Shrimp Pasta, Slow Roasted Lamb Shank, Chipotle NY Strip over Fried Onions, and seven different burgers including Spicy Southwest Burger and Free Range Buffalo Burgers.

But save room for dessert! Try one of the delicious cheesecakes with fresh fruit and chocolate sauce, a sinful Chocolate Confusion Cake (made with seven different chocolates), Greek Baklava, or homemade, authentic Italian Tiramisu.

The family of Christ Barlas has been serving the city of Asheville with great food for more than thirty years. It's his pleasure to share a few favorite recipes, which he enjoys with his own family quite often. He loves the community and appreciates your support!

braised lamb shank with roasted vegetable ragú

Combine the stock, bay leaves and rosemary in a saucepan. Simmer over medium-high heat for 15 to 20 minutes.

Preheat the oven to 350 degrees. Season the shanks with salt, black pepper and red pepper. Dredge in the flour and shake off the excess. Heat olive oil in a Dutch oven or a large heavy ovenproof sauté pan over medium-high heat. Add the shanks and sear for 10 minutes or until a crust forms and the shanks are brown on each side. Remove the shanks to a platter. Add the carrots, celery and onion to the drippings in the Dutch oven. Sauté for 3 to 5 minutes. Add the garlic, tomato paste, oregano and thyme and sauté for 3 to 5 minutes. Add the wine, stirring to deglaze the Dutch oven. Strain the stock, discarding the bay leaves and rosemary. Add the strained stock to the Dutch oven. Crush the tomatoes with your hands and add with the juices to the vegetable mixture. Return the shanks to the Dutch oven. Roast for 1 hour. Turn the shanks over and stir the vegetables. Roast for 1 1/2 hours longer.

8 cups chicken, veal or
   lamb stock
2 bay leaves
1 branch fresh rosemary
4 (16-ounce) lamb shanks
2 tablespoons salt
1 tablespoon coarse black pepper
1 tablespoon crushed red pepper
1/2 cup all-purpose flour
Olive oil for sautéing
1/2 cup coarsely chopped carrots
1/2 cup chopped celery
1 cup coarsely chopped
   yellow onion
3 tablespoons fresh garlic
2 tablespoons tomato paste
1 tablespoon Greek oregano
1 tablespoon thyme
2 cups port or dry red wine
1 (10-ounce) can whole tomatoes

Serves 4

Province 620

chef's table

Province 620

174

marinated citrus salmon with cranberries, mandarin oranges and pecans

Mix the orange juice, pineapple juice, lemon juice and lemon zest in a bowl. Pour over the salmon in a shallow dish. Marinate, covered, in the refrigerator for 1 hour or longer.

Bring the water to a simmer in a saucepan. Stir in the sugar and heat until dissolved. Add the cranberries and cook for 5 to 10 minutes or until the cranberries are about to burst. Remove from the heat and stir in the orange sections and pecans.

Preheat the oven to 350 degrees. Drain the salmon, discarding the marinade. Season the salmon with salt and pepper. Heat the olive oil in an ovenproof grill pan over medium-high heat. Add the salmon and cook for 2 minutes to achieve a nice crust. Turn the salmon over and bake for 7 to 8 minutes depending upon the thickness of the fish, or until the salmon begins to flake. (If you don't have an ovenproof pan, you can finish it on the stovetop.) Top the salmon with the sauce.

Note: This dish is quick and easy, and it creates a little taste of fall. The sauce is quite simple and versatile and can be served over chicken, fish or pork chops.

Province 620

1 cup orange juice
1 cup pineapple juice
Juice and zest of 1 lemon
4 (8- to 10-ounce) salmon fillets
1 cup water
1/2 cup sugar
1 cup frozen or fresh cranberries
1 Mandarin orange,
    cut into sections
1/2 cup pecans
Salt and pepper to taste, or
    blackening seasoning to taste
2 tablespoons extra-virgin
    olive oil

Serves 4

chef's table
mountain flavors

Richmond Hill Inn

Executive Chef

Duane Fernandes

87 Richmond Hill Drive
Asheville, North Carolina 28806
828-252-7313; 800-545-9238
www.richmondhillinn.com
Hours: Dinner is served from
6:00 p.m. – 9:00 p.m.
by reservation only; Wednesday
through Monday evenings.

The dining experience at Richmond Hill Inn is unlike any other in the region. From the Four Diamond Gabrielle's restaurant to afternoon tea; from the sun-filled Ambassador's Grille to the gourmet breakfast, the food and drink of Richmond Hill Inn are certain to delight the palate and stir the soul.

Mornings begin in the Garden Pavilion where guests receive a delicious breakfast with fresh-squeezed juices and beautifully prepared dishes. Afternoons may find guests at the Ambassador's Grille enjoying the magnificent Parterre Garden and marvelous meals. Afternoon tea on the sun porch brings friends together for fresh pastries and teas from around the world. And evenings at Richmond Hill Inn provide a fine dining experience unlike any other, prepared by Executive Chef Duane Fernandes at the award-winning Gabrielle's.

When packing for your stay at Richmond Hill Inn, make sure to include a healthy appetite.

spring asparagus with a "sunny side up" quail egg

Sweat the shallot and garlic lightly in a small amount of olive oil in a small saucepan. Add one-half of the mushrooms and cook until tender. Add the vinegar, stirring to deglaze the saucepan. Add the mushroom stock and bring to a boil. Let cool to room temperature. Process in a blender until blended. Add 1/2 cup olive oil and the truffle oil in a steady stream, processing until emulsified. Season with salt and pepper.

Heat a wide sauté pan over medium-high heat and add a small amount of olive oil. Add the remaining mushrooms and sauté until tender and slightly golden brown in color. Season with salt and pepper.

To serve, lay the asparagus side by side on each of four serving plates. Top with the sautéed mushrooms. Drizzle the vinaigrette around each plate. Place a quail egg on top of the mushrooms and asparagus.

Richmond Hill Inn

1 shallot, thinly sliced
1 garlic clove, thinly sliced
Olive oil for sweating
8 ounces fresh local mushrooms
1/4 cup sherry vinegar
1 cup mushroom stock or water
1/2 cup olive oil
10 drops of truffle oil
Salt and pepper to taste
Olive oil for sautéing
16 asparagus spears, peeled, blanched and chilled
4 quail eggs, cooked sunny side up

Serves 4

chef's table

Richmond Hill Inn

warm sunburst farm-smoked trout tart

Preheat the oven to 350 degrees. Cut the puff pastry into circles using a round cookie cutter. Place between two sheet pans and bake for 5 to 7 minutes or until golden brown. Shave the fennel bulb paper thin using a mandolin. Heat the flaked trout and 1/4 cup crème fraîche gently in a saucepan until warm. Season with salt and pepper. Place on top of the puff pastry rounds neatly, using a ring mold to help form the trout. Toss the shaved fennel, celery leaves, grapefruit, orange and tangerine together in a mixing bowl and place on top of the trout. Garnish with 1/4 cup crème fraîche around the plate to finish.

Richmond Hill Inn

1 sheet puff pastry

1 fresh fennel bulb

1 pound Sunburst Farm hot
   smoked trout, skin removed
   and trout flaked apart

1/4 cup crème fraîche or
   sour cream

Salt and pepper to taste

1/4 cup yellow celery leaves
   (found in the very inner part
   of each bunch)

1 grapefruit, cut into sections

1 orange, cut into sections

1 tangerine, cut into sections

1/4 cup crème fraîche or
   sour cream

Serves 4

chef's table
mountain flavors

Savoy

Owner

Eric Scheffer

641 Merrimon Avenue
Asheville, North Carolina 28804
828-253-1077
www.savoyasheville.com
Hours: Lunch, Monday – Friday
11:30 a.m. – 2:00 p.m.;
dinner, 7 nights a week
5:30 p.m. – until.
AIR member

The Savoy offers international cuisine with world flavors and influences from Italy, Spain, Latin America, and Asia.

Offering the **perfect balance between rich elegance and friendly comfort, the Savoy was** a recent *Santé* Magazine award winner for "Most Innovative Cuisine," "Best Martini Bar," and "Service Excellence in the Southeast."

Menu selections include free-range and hormone-free meats and a variety of fresh seafood that is flown in six days a week from around the world. Everything is made from scratch with only the freshest ingredients.

Owned by a Hollywood producer turned restaurateur, Savoy's proprietor Eric Scheffer brings an air of showmanship and sophistication to Asheville through food, ambiance, and wine. Savoy has been voted "Best Wine List" in Asheville and has won seven *Wine Spectator* Awards of Excellence. "Savoy is a favorite with locals who love great food," reports *Southern Living Magazine.*

garlic mussels

Heat the olive oil and garlic in a skillet over medium heat. Add the tomato and onion and cook until the onion is opaque. Add the wine, stirring to deglaze the skillet. Cook until the mixture is reduced by one-half. Add the lemon juice, rosemary, butter, salt and pepper. Add the mussels and steam until the shells open, discarding any mussels that do not open. Stir with a large spoon to make sure all of the mussels are coated with the liquid.

1/4 cup olive oil
1/2 cup minced garlic
1 cup chopped tomato
1 cup chopped yellow onion
2 cups white wine
1/2 cup lemon juice
3 tablespoons chopped rosemary
6 tablespoons butter
Salt and pepper to taste
4 pounds mussels, scrubbed

Serves 4

peach cobbler

Combine the brown sugar, confectioners' sugar and bourbon in a bowl and mix well. Pour over the peaches in a large bowl. Macerate at room temperature for 6 to 12 hours. Preheat the oven to 350 degrees. Sift the flour, cinnamon and baking powder together. Cream the butter and granulated sugar in a mixing bowl. Add the eggs one at a time, beating well after each addition. Add the crème fraîche and mix well. Add the flour mixture and mix well. Place the peaches and a little of the liquid in a baking dish. Cover with the batter and bake for 15 to 20 minutes or until the topping is golden brown.

12 ounces brown sugar
6 ounces confectioners' sugar
3 cups bourbon
5 pounds peaches, sliced
4 cups all-purpose flour
2 tablespoons cinnamon
2 tablespoons baking powder
1 cup (2 sticks) butter, softened
2 cups granulated sugar
5 eggs
2 cups crème fraîche

Serves 8

chef's table

Savoy

182

gambas al ajio

Heat the oil over medium heat in a sauté pan. Add the garlic, green onions and red pepper flakes. Sauté for 1 minute. Add the shrimp and poach for 3 to 5 minutes or until the shrimp turn pink. Spoon into a serving dish or shallow bowl. Serve hot with the bread for dipping.

Savoy

1¹/2 cups extra-virgin olive oil

¹/2 cup minced garlic

¹/2 cup chopped green onions

¹/3 cup crushed red pepper flakes

16 large shrimp, peeled and deveined

Loaf of fresh bread, sliced and grilled

Serves 4

Davidson and David Vance petitioned the state of North Carolina for the formation of Buncombe County, named in honor of Revolutionary War hero Colonel Edward Buncombe.

chef's table

Souper Sandwich

Chef

Joel Meadows

46 Haywood Street
Asheville, North Carolina 28801
828-285-0002
www.ashevillesoupersandwich.com
Hours: Daily 8:00 a.m. – 5:00 p.m.
AIR member

Souper Sandwich, a downtown favorite since 1994, features breakfast and lunch items as well as catering. It is conveniently located on Haywood Street inside the Haywood Park Hotel atrium.

The restaurant's goal is to offer fresh foods and friendly service while supporting local growers. The famous salad bar features only the freshest produce, as well as hot bar items and homemade soups. Sandwiches are made with only the finest meats and cheeses and served on bakery fresh breads.

If you're looking for baked goods, check out the wide selection of gourmet cookies, muffins, sweet breads, and New York-style bagels—all baked fresh daily.

Enjoy your favorite with a hot cup of freshly brewed coffee offered in a variety of flavors, including seasonal selections and organics, as well as specialty coffees.

tarragon chicken salad

Combine the chicken, celery, almonds, tarragon, bouillon granules and mayonnaise in a bowl and mix well.

6 boneless skinless chicken
 breasts, cooked and
 finely chopped
2 ribs celery, finely chopped
1/2 cup toasted almonds
4 ounces fresh tarragon, chopped
1 teaspoon chicken
 bouillon granules
1 cup mayonnaise

Serves 6 to 8

Stagecoach travel to and from Asheville became established in the 1830s, forming the genesis of the city's reputation as a health resort, summer retreat, and later as a tourist attraction.

chef's table

Souper Sandwich

186

salmon blt

Preheat the grill. Place the salmon on a grill rack and grill until the salmon flakes easily. Cook the bacon in a skillet until crisp. Remove the bacon to paper towels to drain. Melt butter in a skillet. Add the bread and cook until brown and toasty on both sides. Spread the Rémoulade Sauce on one slice of the bread. Layer the lettuce, tomato, salmon and bacon over the sauce. Top with the remaining slice of bread and cut into halves.

8 ounces Atlantic salmon fillet

4 slices bacon with black pepper

Butter for browning

2 slices wheatberry bread

2 ounces Rémoulade Sauce (below)

2 leaves fresh green leaf lettuce

3 slices tomato

Serves 1

rémoulade sauce

Combine the mayonnaise, capers, dill weed, garlic, mustard and lemon juice in a bowl and mix well.

3 1/2 pints mayonnaise

1/4 cup capers

1 ounce fresh dill weed

1/2 ounce garlic, minced

1 ounce stone ground mustard

1/4 cup lemon juice

Makes about 4 pints

chef's table
mountain flavors

South Rock Grille

Chef

Morgan Fiebig

830 Greenville Highway
Hendersonville, North Carolina 28792
828-697-6257
Hours: Monday – Thursday
11:00 a.m. – 1:00 a.m.;
Friday and Saturday
11:00 a.m. – 2:00 a.m.
Hours vary on Sunday.

The foundation of South Rock Grille is based on the family philosophy: "Doing things the right way or not at all."

Owner Morgan Fiebig and her husband, Larry, designed and built the Grille with the help of several employees and their two sons, Graham (dessert chef) and Vaughn (line cook).

Morgan's style of cooking is based on her mother's knowledge of food and world travels, with everything being made from scratch and prepared on a daily basis for freshness. The dining experience is most likely one you will never forget and will want to experience frequently.

south rock chicken

Preheat the oven to 375 degrees. Chop the artichoke hearts and sun-dried tomatoes and mix together in a bowl. Place the chicken on a baking sheet and sprinkle with salt and pepper. Top with the artichoke mixture. Bake for 20 to 30 minutes or until the chicken is cooked through.

Bring the cream and garlic to a boil in a saucepan. Add the basil and reduce the heat. Simmer until thickened, stirring constantly. Place the chicken in a serving bowl. Pour the sauce over the chicken and serve.

1/2 cup canned artichoke hearts
1 cup sun-dried tomatoes
4 (6-ounce) chicken breasts
Salt and pepper to taste
1 cup cream
1 teaspoon chopped fresh garlic
1/4 cup fresh basil

Serves 4

During the Civil War years, North Carolina was the last state to secede from the Union. During the course of the war, North Carolina lost more soldiers—40,000 killed—than any other state.

chef's table

South Rock Grille

190

cobb salad

To prepare the dressing, combine the vinegar, garlic, lemon juice, Worcestershire sauce, salt, pepper, mustard, sugar, vegetable oil and olive oil in a glass jar with a lid. Seal the jar with the lid and shake to mix well.

To prepare the salad, rinse the romaine and green leaf lettuce and pat dry. Tear into bite-size pieces and place in a large bowl. Place the tomatoes, bacon, chicken, chives, blue cheese and avocado in rows across the top. Drizzle with the dressing and garnish with the eggs.

cobb salad dressing

1/4 cup red wine vinegar

1 small garlic clove, pressed

1 teaspoon fresh lemon juice

3/4 teaspoon Worcestershire sauce

2 teaspoons salt

3/4 teaspoon fresh ground black pepper

1/4 teaspoon dry mustard

1/4 teaspoon sugar

3/4 cup vegetable oil

1/4 cup olive oil

salad

1/2 head romaine

1/2 head green leaf lettuce

2 tomatoes, chopped

6 slices bacon, crisp-cooked and chopped

2 chicken breasts, grilled and chopped

3/4 cup chopped chives

1/2 cup crumbled blue cheese

1 avocado, cut into quarters and thinly sliced

2 hard-cooked eggs, cut into halves for garnish

Serves 2

chef's table

Spirits on the River

Owner/Chef

Phillip and Anne Bell

574 Swannanoa River Road
Asheville, North Carolina 28803
828-299-1404
Hours: Wednesday
5:00 p.m. – 9:00 p.m.;
Thursday – Sunday
12:00 p.m. – 9:00 p.m.

Spirits on the River opened in Cherokee in 1988 to serve foods of the Americas and to honor Native American people for their unrecognized primary place in the history of food cultivation. They cultivated an amazing 60 percent of the world's grown foods, which are now spread all over the earth, enabling other cultures to enrich and stabilize their food supplies.

Native Americans taught European Americans the technique of barbecuing foods using various woods and spices. Louisiana Indians taught the French and African-Americans how to cook with chile peppers, sassafras, and beans to create their Cajun and Creole foods. Cherokee Indians educated the European Americans about making grits, hominy, corn bread, and bean bread and showed them ramps, watercress, grassy greens, poke salad, and many, many other foods that helped the newcomers survive.

quinoa cakes **with** avocado red papaya **salsa**

To prepare the cakes, boil the quinoa in water to cover in a saucepan until the grains open wide; drain. Heat the olive oil in a large sauté pan over medium heat. Add the tomato, onion, green onions, bell pepper, cayenne pepper, mushrooms and salt and sauté for 2 minutes. Reduce the heat. Add the quinoa and mix well. Remove from the heat to cool. Shape 4 ounces of the mixture at a time into cakes. Mix the flour and cornmeal together. Coat the cakes with the flour mixture. Heat the peanut oil in a skillet over medium heat. Add the cakes and fry until golden brown on each side, turning once. (You may bake in a 375-degree oven for 20 minutes or until brown.)

To prepare the salsa, combine the tomato, onion, cilantro, jalapeño chile, garlic, cumin, cayenne pepper, salt, papaya and avocado in a bowl and mix well. Spoon over the cakes to serve.

Note: Quinoa is a grain originally from Peru and the Incan Indians held it in high esteeem, calling it the "Mother Grain." Quinoa has more protein in it than any other grain in the world.

cakes

8 ounces quinoa grain

1/2 cup extra-virgin olive oil

1 cup chopped tomato

1 cup chopped sweet onion

1/4 cup chopped green onions

1/4 cup chopped orange bell pepper

1 teaspoon cayenne pepper

1 cup shiitake mushrooms, sliced

1 teaspoon salt

2 cups unbleached self-rising flour

1/2 cup yellow cornmeal

1 cup peanut oil

avocado red papaya salsa

1 cup chopped tomato

1 cup chopped sweet onion

1/4 cup chopped cilantro

1 jalapeño chile, chopped

1/4 cup minced garlic

1 tablespoon cumin

1 teaspoon cayenne pepper

1 teaspoon salt

1/2 cup chopped red papaya

1 avocado, chopped

Serves 6

chef's table

Spirits on the River

buffalo sirloin tips over wild rice

Cut the buffalo sirloin into bite-size pieces. Sauté the buffalo sirloin, mushrooms, tomatoes, Vidalia onions, green onions, garlic, cayenne pepper, salt and black pepper in the clarified butter in a large sauté pan over medium heat until the buffalo sirloin is brown. Serve over the rice.

Note: You may use white or brown rice.

Photograph at left.

1 pound buffalo sirloin
2 cups mixed shiitake mushrooms
    and portobello mushrooms
1 cup chopped tomatoes
1/2 cup chopped Vidalia onions
1/2 cup chopped green onions
2 tablespoons minced garlic
1 teaspoon cayenne pepper
Salt and black pepper to taste
1/2 cup clarified butter
1/2 cup wild rice, cooked

Serves 1 to 2

gator burrito

Sauté the gator meat, 1/4 cup of the tomato, 1/4 cup of the sweet onion, the green onions, garlic, cayenne pepper, salt and black pepper in clarified butter in a medium sauté pan until the gator meat is light in color. Warm the tortilla and place on a plate. Layer the rice and the gator meat mixture on the tortilla and fold up to enclose the filling. Melt the cheese on top of the burrito and place the lettuce, remaining tomato and remaining onion on top.

Note: You may also use brown or white rice and Cheddar cheese.

6 ounces gator tail meat, chopped
1/2 cup chopped tomato
1/2 cup chopped sweet onion
1/4 cup chopped green onions
2 tablespoons minced garlic
Cayenne pepper to taste
Salt and black pepper to taste
Clarified butter for sautéing
1 large tortilla
1/2 cup cooked wild rice
1/4 cup (1 ounce) shredded
    Monterey Jack cheese
Lettuce

Makes 1 burrito

Spirits on The River

chef's table

mountain flavors

Sunny Point

Owners

*April Moon Harper
and Belinda Raab*

626 Haywood Road
Asheville, North Carolina 28806
Call us, we are friendly!
828-252-0055
Hours: 8:30 a.m. – 2:30 p.m.
Sunday and Monday;
8:30 a.m. – 9:30 p.m.
Tuesday through Saturday

"What is our favorite meal of the day?"

That question was posed three years ago to open the doors of Sunny Point Café in West Asheville. Today, the small restaurant has been serving the answer—breakfast—at a breakneck pace.

Sunny Point was conceived as a small, sleepy, neighborhood bakery/restaurant serving items made from local, organic ingredients.

While most ingredients remain local and organic, not much else is the same. Today's focus has shifted to evening dining and the catering business. So, if you crave hot cakes or huevos even at 9 p.m., Sunny Point has you covered.

savory french toast sandwich

Brown the sausage in a skillet, stirring until crumbly; drain. Let cool.

Combine the sausage, cream cheese and Cheddar cheese in a bowl and mix well. Spread 1/4 inch thick on one-half of the bread. Top with the remaining bread.

Mix the milk, cream, eggs, sugar, vanilla, nutmeg and salt in a bowl. Dip each sandwich into the milk mixture to coat and place in a buttered skillet or on a buttered griddle. Cook over medium-low heat until the bread is brown and toasty and the center is hot, turning once. Cut each sandwich into halves and serve with warm maple syrup and fresh fruit.

Sunny Point

1 pound hot breakfast sausage

16 ounces cream cheese, softened

4 cups (16 ounces) white sharp
   Cheddar cheese

1 loaf sandwich bread, sliced
   5/8 to 3/4 inch thick

1 1/2 cups milk

1/4 cup heavy cream

6 eggs

3 tablespoons sugar

1 teaspoon vanilla extract

Pinch of nutmeg

Pinch of salt

Maple syrup

Fresh fruit

Serves 9 to 10

chef's table

Sunny Point

tuna dynamite roll

Bring the rice and 1¹/4 cups water to a boil in a saucepan over medium-high heat. Cover and reduce the heat to low. Cook for 15 minutes. Spoon the rice into a bowl. Add the vinegar and sugar and toss to mix.

Mix the tuna, lime zest, lime juice, sesame oil, sesame seeds, garlic sauce, scallions, mayonnaise and salt in a bowl. Spread the sushi rice with wet hands onto nori sheets. Use a palate knife to make the rice covering very thin and to cover the entire sheet. Spread the tuna mixture along one edge of the sheet and roll toward the opposite edge.

Mix the flour and ³/4 cup water in a bowl to form a paste. Lightly coat the nori rolls with the flour paste and then roll in the panko until completely covered.

Preheat 2 inches of vegetable oil in a Dutch oven to 350 degrees. Place the nori rolls two at a time in the hot vegetable oil and fry until golden brown. Remove from the vegetable oil and drain on paper towels. Cut each roll while hot into six or seven ¹/2-inch slices and serve with wasabi and ponzu sauce.

Sunny Point

1 cup sushi rice
1¹/4 cups water
¹/4 cup rice wine vinegar
2 tablespoons sugar
1 (8-ounce) piece Ahi tuna, cut into ¹/2-inch cubes
Zest of 1 lime
Juice of ¹/2 lime
1 teaspoon sesame oil
¹/2 teaspoon black sesame seeds
1 tablespoon Huy Fong Foods chili garlic sauce
Green portions of 3 scallions, chopped
¹/4 cup mayonnaise
Salt to taste
Sushi nori sheets
1¹/2 cups all-purpose flour
³/4 cup water
4 cups panko (Japanese bread crumbs)
Vegetable oil for frying

Serves 7

chef's table
mountain flavors

Sunset Terrace

Chefs

Kelly Patton and Kingston Clark

Grove Park Inn Resort and Spa
290 Macon Avenue
Asheville, North Carolina
828-252-2711
www.groveparkinn.com
Hours: Lunch Monday – Saturday:
11:00 a.m. – 3:00 p.m.; Sunday:
10:30 a.m. – 3:00 p.m.; Dinner
Nightly, 6:00 p.m. – 9:30 p.m.
AIR member

The Sunset Terrace is the Grove Park Inn Resort and Spa's classic steakhouse, serving prime beef and fresh seafood for dinner and a variety of salads, sandwiches, and entrées for lunch in what is arguably its most breathtaking setting. Western views of the Blue Ridge Mountains come with every entrée, and each is prepared with the type of precision and service that anticipates every one of your taste buds. For the ultimate Sunset Terrace experience, Chef Kelly Patton recommends the Duck Marsala for lunch; for dinner, he recommends the Twin Lamb Rib Chops with balsamic and fresh mint fusion and roasted fingerling potatoes.

The Sunset Terrace is in the Main Inn just outside The Great Hall Bar (inside and adjacent to The Great Hall Bar during inclement weather and/or off season).

trout frangelico

Slightly break up the walnuts. Mix the walnuts, almonds and bread crumbs in a shallow dish. Dredge the trout in the seasoned flour, the egg wash and the bread crumb mixture and set aside.

Sauté the shallot in a small saucepan until caramelized. Add the wine and Frangelico and stir to deglaze the saucepan. Add the thyme and cream. Cook until the mixture is reduced by one-half. Remove from the heat. Add the butter gradually, stirring to mix.

Heat a large saucepan over medium-high heat and add oil. Add the trout breaded side down and cook until golden brown. Turn the trout over and cook until the trout is flaky. We serve with a warm potato salad but any side dish goes well with this dish.

Sunset Terrace

1/4 cup walnuts

1/4 cup almonds

1/4 cup bread crumbs

2 trout fillets, deboned

1/4 cup all-purpose flour, seasoned

1/4 cup egg wash

1 shallot, chopped

1/4 cup white wine

1/4 cup Frangelico

2 sprigs of fresh thyme

1/4 cup heavy cream

*1/2 cup (1 stick) butter,
    cut into slices*

Vegetable oil

Serves 2

chef's table

Sunset Terrace

202

grilled chicken paillard with peach salsa and jalapeño butter

To prepare the butter, pulse the butter, cilantro, jalapeño chile, lime juice, salt and pepper in a food processor or blender until well blended. Shape into a log on a sheet of foil or plastic wrap and roll up to wrap tightly. Freeze for up to two months. Remove from the freezer and cut into 1/2-inch slices as needed.

To prepare the salsa, combine the peaches, bell pepper, onion, parsley, garlic, pineapple juice, lime juice and jalapeño chile in a medium bowl and toss to mix. Cover and chill in the refrigerator for 1 hour or up to 4 days to allow the flavors to blend. Season with salt just before serving.

To prepare the chicken and serve, remove the cartlidge and pound the chicken 1/2 inch thick. Combine the chicken, shallot, oil and lime juice in a glass bowl and toss to coat. Marinate, covered, in the refrigerator for 1 to 2 hours. Preheat the grill or broiler. Place the chicken on a grill rack or on a rack in a broiler pan. Grill or broil for 2 minutes per side or until cooked through. Place a pat of the butter on top of the chicken and serve with the salsa on the side.

jalapeño butter
1 cup (2 sticks) unsalted
* butter, softened*
1 handful cilantro leaves, chopped
1 small jalapeño chile, seeded
* and chopped*
1 tablespoon lime juice
2 teaspoons salt
Freshly ground pepper to taste

peach salsa
2 ripe peaches, pitted and chopped
1 small red bell pepper, chopped
1/2 small red onion, chopped
1/4 cup chopped fresh parsley
1 garlic clove, minced
1/4 cup pineapple juice
6 tablespoons lime juice
1 jalapeño chile, seeded and
* minced*
Salt to taste

chicken
4 chicken breasts, cut into halves
1 shallot, minced
2 tablespoons vegetable oil
Juice of 1 lime

Serves 8

chef's table

mountain flavors

Vincenzo's

Owner

Dwight Butner

10 North Market Street
Asheville, North Carolina 28801
828-254-6498
www.vincenzos.com
Hours: Monday – Thursday
5:00 p.m. – 10:00 p.m.;
Friday and Saturday
5:00 p.m. – 11:00 p.m.;
Sunday 5:00 p.m. – 9:00 p.m.
AIR member

Vincenzo's Ristorante and Bistro is Asheville's premier northern Italian, continental restaurant. Since its opening in 1990, Vincenzo's has established itself as an institution in Asheville's downtown restaurant scene. An abiding commitment to providing customers the finest, most complete evening out has led to numerous awards for outstanding food and excellent service.

Combine that with an elegant yet comfortable atmosphere and live jazz, blues, and standards every night of the week, and you have one of Western North Carolina's finest values. Described by guests as "chic and trendy, yet warm and friendly," Vincenzo's Bistro is a cross between a piano bar and a supper club. Smoking is allowed in the Bistro, and a variety of fine cigars are provided.

Come build some wonderful memories at Vincenzo's Ristorante and Bistro.

pistachio-encrusted trout

Preheat the oven to 350 degrees. Season the trout with salt and pepper. Spray the flesh side of the trout with nonstick cooking spray and press into the chopped pistachios to coat. Coat a hot ovenproof skillet with oil. Place the trout pistachio side down in the prepared skillet and cook until the pistachios are toasted. Add the butter and turn the trout over. Lay the cheese over the trout and bake for 2 minutes.

Note: Caciotta Al Tartufo is sheep and cow mild cheese blend laced with truffle. It is available at the Western North Carolina Farmer's Market.

4 mountain trout, head off and
clear cut
Salt and pepper to taste
8 ounces finely chopped
pistachios
Olive oil for coating
6 tablespoons butter
1 pound Caciotta Al Tartufo,
shaved (see Note)

Serves 4

Vincenzo's

linguini aglio olio pepperoncino

Heat a sauté pan and add the olive oil, kosher salt, black pepper and garlic. Cook until the garlic clears. Stir in the parsley, scallions and red pepper flakes. Add to the hot cooked pasta and toss to coat.

6 tablespoons virgin olive oil
Kosher salt and freshly ground
black pepper to taste
1 ounce fresh garlic, crushed
1 ounce parsley
3 ounces scallions
Red pepper flakes to taste
2 cups linguini, cooked

Serves 1 to 2

chef's table

mountain flavors

Vincenzo's

cotoletta valle d'aosta

Preheat the oven to 400 degrees. Season the veal with salt and pepper and dredge in flour. Dip in egg wash and coat with bread crumbs. Deep-fry in hot oil in a deep-fryer or deep pan until brown. Drain and place on a baking sheet. Lay the prosciutto and cheese over the veal. Bake for 5 minutes.

Dip the butter in flour to coat. Heat a drop of olive oil in a skillet and add the rosemary. Stir in the wine, veal stock, salt and pepper. Add the coated butter and heat to tighten the sauce, stirring constantly. Place the veal on a serving plate and drizzle the sauce over the top.

Note: The dish is named after the Valle D'Aosta region of Italy (above the Piedmont) because of the fontina cheese produced there. It is produced in large 100-gallon vats outdoors on top of the Alps.

1 veal chop
Salt and pepper to taste
All-purpose flour
Egg wash
Bread crumbs
Vegetable oil for deep-frying
2 slices prosciutto
2 slices fontina cheese
2 tablespoons butter
Drop of olive oil
1 sprig of fresh rosemary, chopped
6 tablespoons red wine
6 tablespoons veal stock

Serves 1

Vincenzo's

chef's table

mountain flavors

Weaverville Milling Company

Executive Chef

Jeff Cassanego

1 Old Mill Lane
(off Reams Creek Road)
Weaverville, North Carolina 28787
828-645-4700
www.weavervillemilling.com
Hours: Open at 5:00 p.m. daily.
Closed on Wednesdays.

Friendly hospitality and good food await you at this historic Weaverville Milling Co. Restaurant, north of Asheville in Weaverville off Reems Creek Road—toward the Vance birthplace historic site.

This Buncombe County landmark was a grain mill from 1912 to 1965. Today the Mill has a reputation for fine food in a unique atmosphere. Fresh mountain trout is the Mill's specialty, but it also serves fantastic steaks and chicken, plus a complete menu of many of your favorites. The old-fashioned covered porch is a perfect spot for a relaxing dinner in the spring and summer.

The Mill is open six days a week at 5 p.m. (in season) except for special hours on Easter, Mother's Day, and Thanksgiving starting at noon. Closed on Wednesdays.

pastel (brazilian empanadas)

Heat a skillet over medium-high heat. Brown the ground chuck in the hot skillet, stirring until crumbly. Season with salt and pepper. Remove from the skillet and drain. Heat the olive oil in the skillet over medium heat. Add the onion and sauté for 1 minute. Add the garlic, salt and pepper and cook until the onion is translucent. Add the Worcestershire sauce and red wine vinegar, stirring to deglaze the skillet. Return the ground chuck to the skillet and mix well. Stir in the Sriracha. Remove from the heat to cool. Stir in the hard-cooked eggs and one-half of the beaten eggs and mix well.

Preheat the oven to 350 degrees. Lay out five to ten shells at a time. Brush the edge of each shell with some of the remaining beaten egg. Spoon 1 to 1 1/2 tablespoons of the ground chuck mixture onto each shell. (You want each one full, but not so full that it will tear the dough to fold over.) Fold over each to enclose the filling and seal the edge with a fork.

Line the pastels on a lightly greased baking sheet. Brush each liberally with the remaining beaten egg. Bake for 25 to 30 minutes or until brown. Remove from the oven to cool.

1 to 1 1/2 pounds ground chuck
Salt and pepper to taste
1 tablespoon olive oil
1/2 onion, chopped
3 or 4 garlic cloves, minced
1 1/2 teaspoons Worcestershire sauce
1 1/2 teaspoons red wine vinegar
1 to 2 teaspoons Sriracha, or your favorite hot sauce
4 hard-cooked eggs, chopped
2 eggs, beaten
1 to 2 packages Goya frozen empanada shells, thawed

Makes about 20

Weaverville Milling Company

chef's table

Weaverville Milling Company

210

pork with apple-nut stuffing and plum sauce

To prepare the sauce, drain the plums, reserving the syrup. Remove the pits from the plums and discard. Purée the plums in a blender. Heat the reserved syrup in a large saucepan. Add the sugar, butter, wine and cinnamon stick and mix well. Stir in enough cornstarch to thicken. Add the puréed plums and cook until the mixture is bubbly. (This makes 1/2 gallon and may be stored in the refrigerator. It is also good served over chicken.)

To prepare the stuffing, preheat the oven to 425 degrees. Mix the bread cubes, apples, nuts, garlic, white pepper, poultry seasoning, parsley flakes, apple juice and milk in a bowl. Spoon into a greased 8×8-inch baking pan. Bake for 15 to 20 minutes. Maintain the oven temperature.

To assemble, cut the pork into thin slices. Place 4 cups of the stuffing in a greased 2-quart baking dish. Layer the pork over the stuffing and top with 4 to 5 cups of the plum sauce. Bake for 15 to 20 minutes.

Weaverville Milling Company

plum sauce
1 (3-pound) can whole
   purple plums
1 to 1 1/2 cups sugar
2 tablespoons butter
1/2 cup red wine
1 cinnamon stick (optional)
Cornstarch

apple-nut stuffing
4 cups bread cubes
2 large apples, peeled
   and chopped
1 cup chopped nuts
1 1/2 teaspoons garlic
1 1/2 teaspoons white pepper
1 tablespoon poultry seasoning
1 tablespoon parsley flakes
1/4 cup apple juice
1 to 1 1/2 cups milk

assembly
1 pork tenderloin, cooked

Serves 4

area hot spots

Western North Carolina has miles of trails, mountains, waterfalls, and even America's largest private mansion to explore. In 2003, the U.S. Congress designated the twenty-five westernmost counties as the Blue Ridge National Heritage Area.

Within its 10,514 square miles, there's plenty to see and do, including a visit to America's largest private mansion or spending time with descendants of the continent's first residents at Cherokee.

Penn Dameron, executive director of the heritage area, points out our mountains include the tallest peak east of the Mississippi at Mount Mitchell, the highest waterfall in the Eastern U.S. at Whitewater Falls, the deepest gorge at Linville Gorge, the oldest river in North America—the New River, and the two most visited national parks in the country with the Blue Ridge Parkway and the Great Smoky Mountains National Park.

If you're thinking about eating out, try making restaurants near these top tourism spots part of your visit.

Biltmore

More than one million visitors troop each year through George Vanderbilt's European-inspired chateaux with its impressive art and furnishings and majestic views of the French Broad River and Mount Pisgah in the distance. The 8,000-acre estate features a winery, restaurants, Inn at Biltmore Estate, horseback riding, and more. Admission fee. Call 274-6333 or (800) 295-4730 or visit www.biltmore.com.

The Blue Ridge Parkway

Some twenty million travelers each year wind along the scenic roadway that meanders across the mountains 469 miles from the Shenandoah to the Great Smoky Mountains National Park. In Asheville, the parkway intersects U.S. 25, 70, and 74. Open year-round, weather permitting. Admission is free. Call 298-0398 for automated road and weather conditions. Call parkway headquarters at 271-4779 or visit www.nps.gov/blri.

Great Smoky Mountains National Park

With twenty million visitors each year, it is one of the most visited national parks in the nation. The park extends about seventy miles along the North Carolina-Tennessee border and offers hiking trails, scenic driving routes, horseback riding, camping, and more. Open year-round; admission is free. Call (865) 436-1200 or visit www.nps.gov/grsm.

Cherokee

A sovereign nation to itself, the Qualla Boundary is home to the Eastern Band of Cherokee Indians. While most of the Cherokee were forcibly removed to Oklahoma on the Trail of Tears, a few families hid out in the mountains and were able to keep their claim to their homeland. Visitors can sample the ancient Cherokee heritage with a tour through the renovated Museum of the Cherokee Indian or touring the Oconaluftee Indian Village for demonstrations of ancient crafts. Admission fee. Call (800) 438-1601 or visit www.cherokee-nc.com.

Cradle of Forestry

Located on U.S. 276 four miles south of Milepost 412 on the Blue Ridge Parkway, the Cradle of Forestry features exhibits, films, guided tours, restored historic buildings from the late 1800s and early 1990s, forestry exhibits, a restored steam locomotive, and a gift shop. Nominal fee charged. Open daily 9 a.m. to 5 p.m. starting April 15 through November. Call 877-3130 or (800) 660-0671 or visit www.cradleofforestry.org.

Grandfather Mountain

This private park near Linville features a swinging bridge, hiking trails, and a museum. Preserved by Hugh Morton and his family, the park is also the site to such local events as the Singing on the Mountain and the annual Highland Games and Gathering of the Scottish Clans. Admission fee. Call 733-4337 or (800) 468-7325 or visit www.grandfather.com.

Connemara

The Carl Sandburg Home National Historic Site: three miles south of Hendersonville at Flat Rock. The famed poet and biographer spent his later years on this 263-acre estate with his wife, who raised prize-winning goats. Nominal fee charged; guided tours given daily except Christmas. Call 693-4178 or visit www.nps.gov/carl.

Mount Mitchell State Park

At 6,684 feet in the Black Mountains, Mount Mitchell is the highest peak in North America, east of the Mississippi. The mountain is named for Elisha Mitchell, the academic who explored the peak, but later fell to his death on a nearby waterfall. His grave is on the summit, but the observation tower there is being rebuilt. The park is accessible by N.C. 128 off the Blue Ridge Parkway. The park is open year-round during the day, weather conditions permitting. It's free, but fees are charged for campsites and picnic shelter rentals. Call (828) 675-4611 or visit http://its.unc.edu/parkproject/visit/momi/home.html.

North Carolina Arboretum

At the edge of the Pisgah National Forest a short distance from Interstates 26 and 40 in Bent Creek, a visitor education center, greenhouse complex, gardens, and loop trail are located on 424 acres. Cars are charged $6 every day except Tuesdays, which are free. Call 665-2492 or visit www.ncarboretum.org.

Wheels Through Time Museum

For motorcycle enthusiasts, this 40,000-square-foot museum features 250 rare and vintage motorcycles and automobiles. It's located on U.S. 19 in Maggie Valley. Admission charged. Open daily April through November. Call 926-6266 or visit www.wheelsthroughtime.com.

area microbreweries

Asheville is the capital of craft beer in North and South Carolina. The city is home to at least five brewing companies, the most of any city in either state.

Highland Brewing Co.

42 Biltmore Ave.

299-3370

The craft beer scene began in 1994 with the opening of Highland Brewing Co., the first and now the largest brewer in town. Their ales are sold on draft and in bottles, across the Carolinas, into Tennessee, and through Georgia. While Highland doesn't offer a tasting room or pub, they always welcome visitors at their East Asheville brewery, but call first to set up something.

Asheville Pizza and Brewing

675 Merrimon Ave.

254-1281

Asheville Brewing Co.

77 Coxe Ave.

255-4077

Brewpub restaurants, serving pizzas, burgers, and other food, plus their own line of house beers. The Merrimon location has a discount movie theater, while the downtown Coxe Avenue spot boasts a big patio.

French Broad Brewing

101-D Fairview Road

277-0222

A working brewery near Biltmore Village with a small tasting room and live music starting at 5:30 p.m. Stop by for a cold one, or for tours, call first. Their beers also are sold in taprooms and restaurants around the area.

Green Man Brewing

23 Buxton Ave.

252-5502

A microbrewery that makes the ales served at Jack of the Wood, The Laughing Seed, and other locations. There's a small rustic tasting room that's extremely popular with beer lovers.

Pisgah Brewing

Unit 150, Eastwood Business Park,

Black Mountain

582-7909

A fast-growing brewery about fifteen minutes from downtown Asheville in Black Mountain. Their beers are sold around the area, and they are currently open to the public on Thursday nights (call before visiting).

area theaters

One of the best times to dine out is before or after a show. Asheville and Western North Carolina offer a wide variety of theaters:

Asheville Community Theatre, 35 E. Walnut St., in the heart of downtown performs a wide range of shows. Call 254-1320 or visit www.ashevilletheatre.org.

North Carolina Stage Company, 15 Stage Lane, is a cozy ninety-nine-seat spot featuring professional Equity actors in its mainstage season. The space also is used by many other smaller groups, so there's something happening virtually year-round. Call 350-9090 or visit www.ncstage.org.

The Montford Park Players, at the Hazel Robinson Amphitheatre near the Montford community of Asheville, is famous for its free outdoor Shakespeare productions, but this year's schedule includes other productions, too. The company also does a ticketed production of *A Christmas Carol* each December. Call 254-5146 or visit www.montfordparkplayers.org.

University and college theater can be found at UNC Asheville, Western Carolina University in Cullowhee, Mars Hill College in Mars Hill, and Warren Wilson College in Swannanoa.

Flat Rock Playhouse, Greenville Highway in Flat Rock, forty minutes from Asheville, is North Carolina's official state theater, featuring professional Equity players. The season runs May–December. Call 693-0731 or visit www.flatrockplayhouse.org.

Southern Appalachian Repertory Theatre, in Owen Theatre at Mars Hill College, is a summer operation with professional actors about thirty minutes from downtown Asheville. Call 689-1239 or visit www.sartheatre.com.

Parkway Playhouse, Green Mountain Drive in Burnsville, is another long-established summer theater about one hour from Asheville. Call 682-4285 or visit www.parkwayplayhouse.com.

Haywood Arts Regional Theatre, at the Performing Arts Center in Waynesville, has become one of the mountains' premiere playhouses and has done many shows not performed by other local companies. The mainstage season runs through November. Call 456-6322 or visit www.harttheatre.com.

Unto These Hills, the outdoor drama about the Cherokee, is each summer at Mountainside Theatre in Cherokee. Performances this year continue through August 18. Call (866) 554-4557.

Hendersonville Little Theater, performing in The Barn, on State Street in Hendersonville, does community theater shows. Call 692-1082 or visit www.hendersonvillelittletheatre.org.

Brevard Little Theatre is currently without its own permanent theater, but does shows on the campus of Brevard College in Brevard. Call 884-2587 or visit www.brevardlittletheatre.com.

The Licklog Players perform in the Peacock Playhouse in Hayesville. Call 389-8632 or (877) 691-9906, or visit www.licklogplayers.org.

asheville citizen-times today

Why wait to get today's news tomorrow? Today's *Asheville Citizen-Times* is using the latest technology to streamline consumer access to news around the clock.

The *Asheville Citizen-Times* is mirroring the newspaper industry's transition as it develops new products across diverse media channels to reach consumers any time, anywhere. Always the community watchdog, the *Citizen-Times* is now leveraging its greatest strength: Local news.

"Our readers want to be engaged, influenced, and feel connected with the Western North Carolina experience; they want to know that the newspaper was written with them in mind," says Executive Editor Susan Ihne. "Our goal is to give our readers a reason to come to us every day."

The modern newsroom enables the readers to interact in real time with journalists. Today's *Asheville Citizen-Times* newsroom now contains multimedia journalists who provide the fastest and deepest coverage of stories and issues in print and online. The result of this evolution is more local news content in print and online, as well as more news submitted by the local community and beyond. The print product showcases this with consolidated sections, new features and sections, and expanded local content, the most notable being the "hyper-local" reader-submitted news about local people, communities, schools, and more.

The online channel, Citizen-Times.com, is the most visited Web site in Western North Carolina, averaging more than five million page views each month. To serve readers better, the site now offers a powerful local search engine on every Web page, allowing the user to find everything from recent news articles and events to local restaurants and retailers.

"In short, the *Citizen-Times* is becoming a premier provider of digital and print information and a hub of community interaction through technology," says Jeffrey Green, president and publisher.

just what makes asheville
a delicious destination?

Close your eyes. Imagine you are in a city…more of a neighborhood, really. Not too big. Very hip. Extremely casual. You may be alone, but you immediately feel part of the scene. Your nose twitches and you are pulled to the savory aromas floating from an outdoor café. You are drawn into an inviting cobblestone courtyard filled with bubbly conversation and contented faces. A smile breaks as you realize where you are— Asheville, North Carolina. The smile comes from knowing that every day, breakfast, lunch, dinner, and late night snacks, you have wonderful food adventures within reach. Different atmospheres…chattery, serene, sophisticated, warm as a family dinner. Different culinary styles…nouveau, traditional, fresh, comforting. Different cuisines…Italian, French, German, Irish, Indian, Mexican, Chinese, Thai, Greek, Southern, New England…from the local land and from the sea. Your smile turns up a bit as you realize your dilemma. You want it all. There are just so many delectable choices in Asheville. A sigh of contentment slips from your lips as you realize that yes…Asheville truly is a delicious destination. What a dilemma.

Independent restaurants abound in the Asheville area. The eclectic mix of owner/chefs provide unique personalities and cuisine styles not typically found in cities of Asheville's size. Diners become friends. Restaurants become home. Menus change daily for continuous surprise, or remain the same for comfort and familiarity. Local produce, cheese, and meat find their way onto many tables. Welcome to Asheville… the *delicious* destination.

Asheville Independent Restaurant Association (AIR) formed as a nonprofit group in 2002 to support and promote dining in locally-owned restaurants. Additionally, the association has created a scholarship foundation to lend a financial hand to culinary students gaining education in the field. The sixty or so member restaurants strive to maintain Asheville's unique culinary landscape highlighted throughout the year with events such as A Taste of Asheville, Chef's Showcase, Main Course Dining, and this cookbook. You are invited to join our wonderful chefs in their kitchens to learn how to make many of the most favored dishes of Asheville's independent restaurants.

For a glimpse into many of Asheville's locally-owned restaurants, visit AIRasheville.org, the Web site of Asheville Independent Restaurant Association.

Index

chef's table

order information

chef's table

mountain flavors from asheville's most celebrated chefs

is available for purchase

for $24.99 plus applicable North Carolina state tax, shipping, and handling.

Using a credit card you may order it online at

www.citizen-times.com/cookbook

using our secure credit card ordering system.

You may stop by the *Asheville Citizen-Times* office during our

regular business hours (Monday – Friday, 8:30 a.m. – 5 p.m. EST)

at 14 O. Henry Avenue, Asheville, North Carolina 28801.

We also accept personal checks payable to *Asheville Citizen-Times*

(please note on the check that you are purchasing a cookbook).

Please call to verify your shipping costs at (828) 232-5934,

and mail checks to P.O. Box 2090, Asheville, North Carolina 28802.